Is God Calling
You to Ministry?

Collegium Books

Mark David Shaw

Destiny Series

Is God Calling You to Ministry?
by Mark David Shaw

Destiny Series

ISBN 978-0-9801865-0-5

Copyright © 2009 by Mark David Shaw

Published by Collegium Books
PO Box 6885
Rochester, MN 55903

To reach us on the Internet:

www.5fold.org
www.collegiumbibleinstitute.com

Is God Calling
You To Ministry?

*"Every Saint Should Be a
Disciple in Order to
Accomplish the Purpose and
Destiny for Which They Were
Created"*

Acknowledgements

I would like to acknowledge the following people who without their help this work would not exist.

Of course, I must thank my God, my Lord Jesus who is the revelator of all things true. The relationship that God has afforded man through the sacrifice of His Son is nothing short of extraordinary.

I would like to thank my wife, Kathryn, who relentlessly motivated me to accomplish this work. Without her planning, encouragement, and critical review this work would not be here at this time. She believed in me and that what I had to say was important enough to put into print. You have shown me the importance of love for our fellow human beings. You have taught me the art of fairness and justice. Thank you for being a partner in life, love, and ministry. I love you for your wisdom, your counsel, and your spirit.

I want to thank my students whose hunger for the Word of God has challenged me to study and go deeper in the entire curriculum.

Thank you Jennifer Zemple for your proofing, suggestions, and all of your hard work.

I want to thank my dad who gave me such a great foundation and by his example made it possible for me to accomplish this work. You are a rock of influence in my life and I would not have reached this milestone without it.

My mother who taught me to believe that I could accomplish anything to which I set my hand, I am eternally grateful.

Dr. Roger Parlin for his influence and mentorship. The many doctrinal conversations served to make me think and study to prove what truth is.

Rev. Shirley Smith who showed me the art of preaching and humility. She was a very early influence in my life, especially as I watched her suffer a terrible pain. I learned a life's worth of lessons from her. Create

Table of Contents

Introduction

Are You Called

This is a biblical look at our callings. Its purpose is to get you to see that you really do have a call. By understanding that God has a purpose for your life, you are empowered to surrender to that call. This chapter will guide the student to seek training in the respective fields of calling to facilitate growth and maturity.

Your Dream is Bigger Than You

The purpose of this chapter is to take the reader on a journey to look realistically at their calling and their inability to finish it without the help of your Creator. It is a motivational chapter that seeks to remove those roadblocks that usually trip us all up in pursuit of destiny.

Mentoring

The objective of this chapter is to prepare the student for discipleship; to understand the roles of disciple and leader; to learn the responsibility that the leader has toward the student and the responsibility the student has toward the leader. The underlying message of this chapter is intended to build the relationship between disciple and leader.

What Role Does Doctrine Play?

This course shows the relationship doctrine has with discipleship. There is a hostile environment with regard to doctrine in many charismatic churches. We deal with this and show the absurdity of demeaning doctrine.

Replicating the Anointing

The goal of discipleship is to replicate the anointing that Jesus passed down to His disciples. We show what is necessary for the disciple and the leader to do that would result is transference of anointing. We seek to bring back the greatest loss the Church has ever known, discipleship.

Identity vs. Individualism

Identity is by far the greatest possible goal for the purpose of accomplishing one's calling. Without a true sense of identity, the disciple will be ill equipped to fulfill their destiny. However, individualism seeks to mask itself as identity and causes the disciple to derail from their true purpose.

The Glory of God is Shriveling

In this chapter, we will show that each Christian is a bearer of the glory of God. The student will learn what the definition of the glory of God is, and what it means to carry that glory within them. It also deals with how this glory can be diminished in the life of the Christian. The goal of this chapter is make the student aware of their importance in God's kingdom and give them the knowledge that would help them to take their proper place in displaying the glory of God.

How Can I Be More Brilliant?

In this chapter, we discuss how we can increase the glory of God in our lives. We show the student that God takes us through a process that produces more glory in our lives. The student will learn to surrender to this process rather than to resist it. It also prepares the student to be encouraged in difficult times. It shows the connection between life traumas and how they cause obstaclesto reaching your full potential.

Communicating With God

Prayer, at its most simplistic definition, is a communication directed toward God. However, it is not supposed to be a singly directed conversation. God indeed speaks to His own and in order to hear Him we must tune ourselves to hear Him.

DESTINY SERIES 101

Are You Called?

Chapter One

I hope to reveal to you that every person is called; also, I hope to show you that which prepares you and qualifies you to operate in these callings. The first thing that I want you to observe is that no matter what you or anyone else thinks, you have a calling. We can either submit to that calling, or we can reject it, but that will not change it nor will it nullify it.

"In the beginning, God created..." Those five words say so much about you and I. Note that for a thing to be created, that creation necessitates that the thing created also has purpose and destiny. This is the great evil advanced in Darwinism, naturalism, or evolution. In the model proffered by evolution, everything is a result of chance.

Under that model, your purpose and value can be no greater than a rock that also exists by chance. To be here by chance means that there is no meaning behind your existence. However, under this idea there is a premium on surviving. The reason being that without purpose for existence, existence becomes the sole purpose of life. That leads to the philosophy of survival of the fittest.

We can see this evil mindset in the beliefs of those that have a naturalistic worldview. You will find that they usually devalue human life and put it on a par with animal life. Why? It is because if evolution is true, then every living thing has just as much value as any other living thing.

If one has a biblical worldview, then they look to what the Creator says about the different living things. Jesus reveals to us that we are indeed much more valuable than the animals.

> *Matthew 10:31 "So do not fear; you are **more valuable** than many sparrows."*

> *Matthew 12:12 "How much **more** valuable then is a man than a sheep! So then, it is lawful to do good on the Sabbath."*

> *Luke 12:24 "Consider the ravens, for they neither sow nor reap; they have no storeroom nor barn, and yet God feeds them; how much **more valuable** you are than the birds!"*

In these Scriptures, we find that Jesus affirms mankind is much more valuable than animals. Why is this important? It is important because of **Who** said these things. You see, because Jesus is also the Creator, He has the right and the power to assign value to His creation.

> *Colossians 1:16-17 **For by Him all things were created**, both in the heavens and on earth, visible and invisible, whether thrones or dominions or rulers or authorities—all things have been created through Him and for Him. He is before all things, and in Him all things hold together.*

Since Jesus is the Creator of all things, then His words hold the greatest of weight concerning our value as humans. He has placed us higher than any other created living physical thing. His words have great import, but His actions reveal a value even greater than words could express. The Creator of all things gave His life for all of mankind! What a tremendous value that Jesus, the Creator, has placed upon you and I!

Our Call

The next thing I want you to perceive is that no matter what you or anyone else thinks; you do have a calling. Everyone has one and it is given by God to fulfill what He wills in our life. We can either submit to that calling or reject it, but that will not dismiss it, invalidate it, disqualify us, or take it away.

> *I Corinthians 12:4-7 Now there are varieties of gifts, but the same Spirit. And there are varieties of ministries, and the same Lord. And there are varieties of effects, but the same God who works all things in all persons. But to each one is given the manifestation of the Spirit for the common good.*
>
> *Romans 11:29 for the gifts and the calling of God are irrevocable.*

I want to look at this verse closely. Notice the mention of the trinity. Father, Son, and Spirit are all presented as active in our callings.

- *"Now there are varieties of gifts, but the same Spirit."* The Spirit distributes the gifts that each person is to have.

- *"And there are varieties of ministries, and the same Lord."* The Son distributes the office of ministry that may be one of the five fold ministries or one of many other callings that we will discuss later.

- *"And there are varieties of effects, but the same God who works all things in all persons."* The Father is the One that gives the combinations and effects of gifts and ministry that the Son and the Spirit give.

- *"But to **each one** is given the manifestation of the Spirit for the **common good**."* The manifestation is the outward demonstration of your gifts and calling. This means that everyone is called and gifted.

From those two Scriptures, we can see that, one, we are ALL called and we all have gifts, and two, these callings and gifts can never be revoked or withdrawn. Therefore, if you refuse to operate in your calling, you will go to the grave with that calling and the gifts that go with it, but never do you lose your calling or your gifts. When you stand before your Creator as a believer, you will have to give an account for the fulfillment of your calling. We have an example clearly shown in the Bible of one who was called, yet did not fulfill that call.

> *Luke 6:13 And when day came, He called His disciples to Him and chose twelve of them, **whom He also named as apostles:***

We know that Jesus being incarnate is God and cannot lie, so we must conclude that the disciple Judas really did have the call of an apostle upon his life. From this we can deduce that one can be called to an office of ministry and yet not fulfill that calling in disobedience to God.

Acts 1:16-17 "*Brethren, the Scripture had to be fulfilled, which the Holy Spirit foretold by the mouth of David concerning Judas, who became a guide to those who arrested Jesus. "For he was counted among us, and **received his portion in this ministry.**"*

Even the other eleven apostles did not begrudge Judas of his appointed place with them. They recognized his calling and place in ministry along side of theirs. Nevertheless, Judas failed to move into his calling and instead chose to listen to that father of lies. Therefore, Judas went to his grave without fulfilling his calling. This same Judas went out two by two in order to heal the sick, cast out demons, and preach the kingdom of God.

When Does One's Calling Take Place?

*Ephesians 2:10 For we are His workmanship, created in Christ Jesus for good works, which God **prepared beforehand**, that we should walk in them.*

From this verse, we can see that our calling was *planned in advance* of our arrival. That means that we are called from the womb, God knows our lives and He has an assignment for each one of us. Think about this; God planned an assignment for you before you ever existed. Your life has a purpose, it has a goal, and it has a direction because of your Creator. Yet, you possess a free will and can chose as Judas did, NOT to walk in the anointing of God's plan for your life.

A thing created is best at doing that for which it was created. A screwdriver is great for inserting or removing screws. You can use a screwdriver to pry with, but it is not as good as a pry bar.

You can use a screwdriver to scrape with, but it will not work as good as a scraper blade.

You too, are best at doing the assignment that you were created to do. You can do other things, but you will not know true fulfillment until you do the thing for which you were created. You will never truly be happy until you walk in that calling of which you are called. This is where you find genuine peace and life satisfaction.

YOUR ASSIGNMENT PRECEDES YOU AND YOUR ASSIGNMENT BECOMES YOU. Ask God to reveal your assignment to you. Then do nothing without first consulting with God. That is, you pray about the decision, you ask God for direction, and you follow what He tells you. The direction that He leads you will always be one of peace and in line with His Word, which is without regard to the outcome. In other words, no matter how daunting the outcome looks, even death, you will have the peace of God if you are walking in His will.

God's grace is only available within the boundaries of those areas that He has called you to walk. In other words, God's grace to do is only available in **obedience**. Every time a person walks away from their calling, they walk away from God's grace, God's favor, God's protection, and God's hand! We are not talking about the grace of God's salvation upon your life, but rather the grace of a calling and all the benefits associated with it.

God uses everybody that is in His family. It does not matter what you feel are your limitations; God is not limited by them. With the Holy Spirit dwelling in you, your potential is unlimited. He uses bound, free, blind, deaf, black, white, Jew, Gentile, male, and female. If you are a human and you are in His family, God uses you. God has a special place and calling for each person in His family, and that makes each one of us unique and special.

> *I Corinthians 7:7 Yet I wish that all men were even as I myself am. However, each man **has his own gift** from God, one in this manner, and another in that.*

You cannot use the excuse that you have no gifts. If you do, according to the Word you are a liar. God gifts us all for a particular purpose. It can only make sense that true contentment, real happiness, real peace, and real joy can only be achieved in that activity for which God created you.

Review:

- Every person is gifted by God.

- Every person is called by God.

- God's gifting and calling can never be revoked.

- God planned a call specifically for your life and this was done before you even came to exist.

How Do We Know What Our Callings Are?

Your designed call is something that is recognizable by the gifts that God has given you. You should notice that even from childhood God has given you gifts that are in agreement with your life, your personality, and your calling. Some of these gifts are given to you from birth; others are given by the Spirit after you become a Christian. These gifts you may not identify as being from God for His purpose, but I assure you that they are.

Since you were created for a specific purpose, you most likely will find that you are already doing things by nature that fit your call and gifts. You may be doing them for different reasons than what God had intended, but you will probably find that you are doing them.

For instance, God called me to the office of teacher. Now I could be a teacher in a secular college or school and be using the gifts and call of God to promote false truths like evolution. God's intention was for me to teach His Word; that is why He gave me that call and gift. Another person may have the gift of music and be using it to glorify the devil rather than God.

In order to find and do what God called you to do, you must surrender to God and to whatever it is that He has assigned you to do. You may be in the beginning stages of that calling, but you should be able to recognize it once you learn about the different callings God has given.

Let me say this because it is vitally important. You **CANNOT** know the totality of what your gifts and callings are **UNLESS** you have **SURRENDERED** your will and your life to God. You can go through your Christian walk without having peace or contentment, always feeling like something is missing in your walk and never satisfied simply because you have not given yourself to God's intention wholly and completely.

Someone may have recognized your calling and told you what it was, but **YOU** will not experience it until you surrender to it. God cannot work through a person that refuses to surrender to His will. Oh, you may do **some** things for God, but your potential is vastly underachieved by not surrendering to the complete work of His calling.

How Do I Cultivate My Calling?

When the five-fold ministries, whose job it is to equip, teaches the different callings mentioned in the Bible, it gives you a framework that will help you to confirm what God has called you to do. One's calling is an inner burning and is best defined by God. Our Father has so established that we should get confirmation and training from His ministers. The reason for this is that God has called and gifted ministers to be able to identify and equip you in your calling. Your responsibility then is to position yourself in the place God is calling you in order to be trained and equipped by His servants.

How Do We Get The Proper Training?

Everyone needs to be a disciple or a student before embarking upon their assignment. This means that you are going to have a leader or mentor that helps to refine your character and define those things God has placed in you. This minister's responsibility is to educate and train you in the area to which God is drawing you.

This is the assignment of the five fold ministry (apostles, prophets, pastors, teachers, and evangelists). That is, they (the ministers) are to recognize your calling as you sit under their ministry, and they are to train and build you up in your calling that you may operate according to the will of God in your life and accomplish His will.

*Ephesians 4:11-16 And He gave some as apostles, and some as prophets, and some as evangelists, and some as pastors and teachers, for the **equipping** of the saints for the work of **ministry**, to the **building up** of the body of Christ; until we all attain to the unity of the faith, and of the knowledge of the Son of God, to a **mature** man, to the **measure** of the **stature** which belongs to the fullness of Christ. As a result, we are no longer to be children, tossed here and there by waves, and carried about by every wind of doctrine, by the trickery of men, by craftiness in deceitful scheming; but speaking the truth in love, we are to grow up in all aspects into Him, who is the head, even Christ, from whom the whole body, being fitted and held together by that which every joint supplies, according to the proper working of each individual part, causes the growth of the body for the building up of itself in love.*

We see from this Scripture that it is the minister's job to equip God's people. What is the minister to equip them to do? God's people are to do THE WORK OF GOD that culminates in BUILDING UP THE BODY OF CHRIST.

Definition – *Equipping*

The Greek word is **katartismos**. (kat-ar-tis-mos)

According to Enhanced Strong's Lexicon it means, *"complete furnishing, equipping."*

According to Vine's Expository Dictionary it means, *"a making fit, implying a process leading to consummation, a fitting or preparing fully."*

According to *"A Greek-English Lexicon of the New Testament and Other Early Christian Literature,"* it means, ***"setting of a bone."***

According to *"Greek-English Lexicon of the New Testament based on Semantic Domains"* it means *"to make someone completely adequate or sufficient for something - to furnish completely, to cause to be fully qualified, adequacy."*

At its root is the idea of setting a bone, thus making functional that part of the body that was dysfunctional. Putting that into context, people start out broken and dysfunctional in their assignment. Equipping them brings them into functionality concerning their calling. It takes that which is broken, sets it or repairs it, and then facilitates healing.

Definition – *Ministry*

The Greek word is **diakonia**. (dee-ak-on-ee'-ah)

According to *Enhanced Strong's Lexicon* it means, *"1) service, ministering, esp. of those who execute the commands of others 2) of those who by the command of God proclaim and promote religion among men 2a) of the office of Moses 2b) of the office of the apostles and its administration 2c) of the office of prophets, evangelists, elders etc. 3) the ministration of those who render to others the offices of Christian affection esp. those who help meet need by either collecting or distributing of charities 4) the office of the deacon in the church 5) the service of those who prepare and present food. "*

This Greek word is that same word used in Acts that we quoted earlier describing Judas' rejection of his ministry.

Definition – *Building Up*

The Greek word is **oikodome**. (oy-kod-om-ay)

According to *Enhanced Strong's Lexicon* it means, *"1) (the act of) building, building up 2) metaph. edifying, edification 2a) the act of one who promotes another's growth in Christian wisdom, piety, happiness, holiness 3) a building (i.e. the thing built, edifice)"*

According to *Vine's Expository Dictionary* it means, *"a building, or edification; of a local church as a spiritual building, or the whole Church, the Body of Christ, **It expresses the strengthening effect of teaching**, or other ministry, (the idea conveyed is progress resulting from patient effort). "*

According to *Greek-English Lexicon of the New Testament based on Semantic Domains* it means, *"the construction of something, with focus on the event of building up or on the result of such an event - **'to build up, to construct,** construction. "*

Definition – *Mature*

The Greek word is **teleios**. (tel'-i-os)

> According to *Enhanced Strong's Lexicon* it means,
> *"1) brought to its end, finished 2) wanting nothing
> necessary to completeness 3) perfect 4) that which
> is perfect 4a) consummate human integrity and
> virtue 4b) of men 4b1) full grown, adult, of full age,
> mature"*

> According to *Vine's Expository Dictionary* it
> means, *"having reached its end, finished, complete,
> perfect."*

> According to *Liddell, H. G., and Scott, Abridged
> Greek-English Lexicon* it means, ***"perfect in his or
> its kind."***

> According to *Greek-English Lexicon of the New
> Testament based on Semantic Domains* it means,
> *"pertaining to being mature in one's behavior -
> 'mature, grown- up.' to the mature person, also
> means maturity of behavior"*

So literally, *"teleios"* is being **functionally perfect**. Let me
give you an example of being functionally perfect. A screwdriver
may have nicks in the handle, a bent shank, and paint stains on it,
but it still functions perfectly according to the purpose for which it
was created.

Definition – *Measure*

The Greek word is **metron**. (met'-ron)

According to *Enhanced Strong's Lexicon* it means,
*"1) measure, an instrument for measuring 1a) a
vessel for receiving and determining the quantity of
things, whether dry or liquid 1b) a graduated staff
for measuring, a measuring rod 1c) proverbially,
the rule or standard of judgment 2) determined
extent, portion measured off, measure or limit 2a)
the required measure, the due, fit, measure"*

Definition – *Stature*

The Greek word is helikia. (hay-lik-ee'-ah)

According to *Enhanced Strong's Lexicon* it means,
*"1) age, time of life 1a) age, term or length of life
1b) adult age, maturity 1c) suitable age for
anything 1d) metaph. of an attained state fit for a
thing 2) stature, i.e. in height and comeliness of
stature."*

According to The *Theological Dictionary of the
New Testament* it means, *"1. This word first means
"age," especially of maturity, collectively
"contemporaries." 2. It then means "generation."
3. A final sense is "physical size," "growth,"
though this does not occur in the papyri, where the
word often has the legal sense of "maturity."*

Let us now put this into perspective.

The fivefold ministry is given for the purpose of:

1. Completely furnishing and equipping the saint; making fit; which makes them completely adequate or sufficient

for the work of:

2. Service or ministry

so that it will result in:

3. The strengthening; the construction; the building up of

the body of Christ: Till we all attain to the unity of the faith, and of the knowledge of the Son of God to:

4. Bring a person to the end of training; to finish them; to make them functionally perfect; to mature them in their behavior

to the point of:

5. Becoming a vessel of measure

for receiving:

6. The total fullness of Christ

so that they will not be deceived by false teachings and teachers.

What is supposed to take place in the realm of Christianity is ministers making ministers, making ministers, making ministers, etc., etc., etc. That is how the Body of Christ is built; that is how we understand and operate in our callings. Let me clarify something. When I use the word *"minister,"* I am using it as an all-inclusive title. Not all are called to one of the offices of the fivefold (apostles, prophets, evangelists, pastors and teachers). All who hold a position in the fivefold are ministers, but not all ministers are in the fivefold. The word *"minister"* simply means *"servant,"* and we are all servants of Christ.

We need to be in training to do God's work. That is partly why we assemble as Christians. Of course, we are to come together for praise, worship, and prayer. Yet, there should be the plan of training and equipping the members to do the work of God in their respective fields. Not only that, but students need a safe platform from which to practice until they are ready to go out and build upon their ministry.

I am afraid that what we see predominantly in the Christian church today is a system **designed around safety**. This is a system that tries to eliminate loose cannons by not training anyone, or at best just a few choice members. It is a safe system designed to keep both the numbers and the finances steady as well. After all, if people are being trained for ministry, what happens when they are ready? They are sent out! This was the vision that Christ had for His Church! We were all commissioned for a calling, and it is the ministers' job to recognize those callings and to help train you in them.

Progression, Regression, or Stagnation

> *Hebrews 5:11-14 Concerning him we have much to say, and it is hard to explain, since you have become dull of hearing. **For though by this time you ought to be teachers, you have need again for***

someone to teach you the elementary principles of
the oracles of God, and you have come to need milk
and not solid food. For everyone who partakes only
of milk is not accustomed to the word of
righteousness, for he is a babe. But solid food is for
the mature, who because of practice have their
senses trained to discern good and evil.

We are all commissioned to study and learn so that we would
be the workers that God wants us to be. It takes effort; it takes
work; it takes patience; however, it should not be a burden to you.
If it is burdensome, then something is out of balance. The desire to
be trained should be strong in you. It will not be easy, but it should
be satisfying. When we are doing what we love to do, then no
matter how hard it is, it is not a burdensome task to us.

Paul received his training from Jesus through revelation and
then served as a teacher in the church at Antioch to finish his
training. Paul also went to Peter to be recognized in his calling.
God has not changed; He can and does train us by revealing His
wisdom and knowledge to us. However, we cannot dismiss the
process that He put in place to mature the saints, which is the
equipping ministry. Whatever it takes, God will equip you to do
His will if you surrender your life to Him.

Jesus trained His disciples who then became apostles; they in
turn trained others, who then trained others. We, on the other hand,
have divorced training from the local church and put that
responsibility on schools or colleges. I am not against colleges. It
would be wonderful to have more of them, but they are not
accessible to everyone in the church. Every church is to be a
training center.

We have put a premium on degrees rather than on training. You see, your spiritual training goes beyond knowledge. A PhD does not make you a mature Christian, or a vessel of measure that is able to receive the fullness of Christ. You can be full of the knowledge of God in your mind and still lack character maturation. The ministers that are responsible for your biblical training are also responsible for your character training.

College alone cannot give you this. It is not that they do not want to, but that they are unable. How can you have a person on staff for every ten to twelve students? True spiritual discipleship takes an abundance of time and effort. The mentor becomes a father or mother to the disciple. The relationship between them has the necessity of closeness **for the reason of character maturation**. There is a reason why Jesus had twelve primary disciples. A person can only pour themselves into a limited number of people at a time.

What qualified the twelve disciples for the office they held? One, it was that they were discipled by Jesus. Their relationship to Jesus was one where He was able to get intimately familiar with their lives and speak to them concerning their behavior. School alone cannot do that for you. Two, their work testified to their calling.

> *I Corinthians 9:2 If to others I am not an apostle, at least I am to you; for you are the seal of my apostleship in the Lord.*

As a result of this system of schools apart from the Church being adopted for the qualifying of ministers, there are many who go through the academic training for ministry, but they lack the maturity and character to operate as ministers. On the other hand, many are trained by their local pastors on a personal level and are not accepted as ministers because they have not been to the accredited schools. Hence, these people specifically trained by local pastors often do possess the maturity of character and knowledge of God to be ministers. What we need to do is to marry the education system back to the church and make it accessible to all in the church.

Man has taken a system that is clearly outlined in the Bible and he changed it into a system that he can control rather than allowing God to control it. Being a minister is a calling; it is not something that one chooses to do as a vocation; it is something that God elects you to be.

What Would The Ideal Church Look Like?

There would be more than just one minister. Each minister would be operating in the calling that Jesus called him or her to do. Each minister would also submit themselves to all the other ministers. This means that the ministers would defer to each of the other's gifts. Ideally, the church would have all five of the callings of the fivefold ministry operating in that body. Rather than a hierarchical order, there would be a college of co-equal ministers.

Those that felt the call of God to sit under this ministry would have their purpose and call recognized, which would then result in their training according to what their calling is. They would be allowed to operate under the tutelage of the other ministers so they would not only develop and increase in the knowledge of God, but also they would develop in character. The church would have an education system that would equip the believer to do the work of God with a curriculum that has the quality of a college education. There would be different levels of training to accommodate the students who are at different levels.

In all of this, everyone would be responsible to witness to the lost. Both those that are the ministers and those who are being trained to minister would witness not only in church, but also in the marketplace of everyday life. This would be an ideal situation and it is sadly a rarity in the local church today.

Two Veins of Training

We are not all called to one of the offices of fivefold ministry. There are other callings as well. We see gifts of helps and gifts of government mentioned in the Bible. We also see gifts of healing and miracles. We see the calling of deacons and overseers. There are many gifts and callings, but there is only one God who gives as He wills to His people. There are many different fields and careers that need the integrity of mature Christian people. There are callings to law enforcement, medical care, manufacturing, and politics. We need Christians in every field of work.

One system of training would facilitate the ordination of ministers who would become equippers themselves. Since not everyone is called into one of the offices of the five ministries mentioned in Ephesians 4:11, there needs to be a system of education tailored to meet the needs of those called into other areas of life. This other system of training would equip the believers who are called into the various fields and careers of this world so that they could take Jesus into these areas in a credible and valid way.

Our problem, though, is this. How can the work of God be accomplished when the few ministers that we do have are stuck ministering in a system that restricts them from making disciples? You see, disciples were not meant to be disciples for life. At some point you stop being the student and you become the teacher. At some point Jesus stopped referring to His disciples as disciples and started calling them apostles.

By that, I do not mean that you stop learning; none of us ever stops learning unless we disengage ourselves. There should always be measurable progress in your walk with God. You were not created continually to be a disciple. You are unique to God and to this world. You have gifts that the rest of us need. God wants to make you into the image that He had in your creation. Yield to Him and humble yourself before Him and He will exalt you.

Conclusion

Since we are all called, it behooves us all to seek to identify our calling and our giftings, begin training and exercise, and begin to live our lives doing what God destined for us to do. The beginning is always surrender; so, surrender your life to God's calling and enter into a life of adventure coupled with the fruits of the Spirit.

Your Dream is Bigger than You

Chapter Two

I think this is probably the most important message I could deliver to any person if they had one message to hear and that is all they had to hear other than salvation. Because in the course of our lives we have a tendency to direct our paths and we go in places that oftentimes God didn't bring us to. When we do that, we are thwarting what God has planned for our life and it creates a situation where we are not emotionally capable or happy. When you see what God has created you to do and you begin to walk in it, you find emotional wholeness. You find wholeness in life. You find satisfaction in life.

I am going to begin by sharing a poem with you. When I first read this poem, I said, *"You know I have to admit, I am not someone who reads poetry and gets a lot out of it."* However, when I read this poem, I said, *"There's something deeper here than what's on the surface."* Therefore, I read it and I re-read it and I re-read it and I re-read it and I was stunned that an eleven-year-old girl could communicate this deep of a message to the Body of Christ.

My Dream Is Bigger Than I
By -Akiane

Romancing white lighthouses
and dusting the nectar of air,
The seagulls freeze

my consciousness lead.
There is no flight beneath the wings –
The flight is ahead.

I ignore the sky cut up with clouds,
For dreams ignite
from the storms in my mind,
Daisies inside raindrops
fill up the winking eye of the childhood,
and I pull down the child's hood.

The unborn dream of growth struggles.
The born struggle to dream.
But I refuse all choices
in exchange
for impossibility.
Only a dirt road
is without any speed limit.

Releasing a young bird
from a solid cliff
for the first time
even the smallest feather
learns how to fly.
And measuring myself I kiss my wishes.
But my dream is bigger than I.

Akiane Kramarik--
Internationally recognized Child
Prodigy- Artist-Poet-, Poem taken
from My Dream is Bigger Than I, by
Akiane Kramarik Age 11

This poem really touched me. Too many times I have witnessed individuals constrain their lives to be so removed from what God has designed for them that it breaks my heart. I listen to all of the negative epoch making moments and how those moments have conditioned them to fail. That is why I titled this chapter, *"Your Dream is Bigger than You."* Your dream really is bigger than you are! Your life does have purpose and you are called. How do we know that? How do we know that we have purpose?

That answer to that question is the difference between a naturalistic worldview and a biblical worldview. A naturalistic worldview says that you are an accident; that you are here by happenstance. If you are an accident, you cannot possess a purpose. Accidents cannot produce purpose, but if you are created, then God created you for a particular reason.

You are not just here because your mother and father had a baby. There is much more to your life than just the idea of random existence. There is more to you than what you can see when you look in a mirror. There is much more to you. You are a spirit being, God created that spirit, He put it within your body, and you became a unique individual with a unique set of skills with a unique purpose.

> **Romans 8:28** *And we know that God causes all things to work together for good to those who love God, to those who are **called according to His purpose.***

Romans 8:28. It is a familiar scripture to many. Although, I have to wonder how many actually see themselves in the last part of that verse. We know that God loves us all. Yet, do we actually know that God calls us all and we are not just called, but we are called according to His purpose? That means when He created your spirit He wove into your spirit the necessary talents and gifts to carry you to your destiny. Think about that. Your existence, which comes from the Holy One, the Almighty God, is actually proof of your call.

> *II Timothy 1:9 who has saved us and **called us** with a holy calling, not according to our works, but **according to His own purpose** and grace which was granted us in Christ Jesus from all eternity,*

Part of the problem in understanding your calling is that sometimes you may think, *"I can't do this." "What do you mean I'm called?" "How am I going to accomplish it?" "What am I going to do?" "I thought that all I had to do was go to church?"* Well that is where the Church is supposed to help. The Body of Christ is supposed to be a guide to the blind. When people come in and they are blind, they do not know where they belong and they do not know to what calling they are called. It is our job to help them along, to bring them to that place. In fact, your calling actually existed before you existed.

> *Ephesians 2:10 For we are His workmanship, created in Christ Jesus for good works, **which God prepared beforehand** so that we would walk in them.*

God prepared the work for you to do before He created you. The work existed before you got here and God created you, put your spirit in you, and gifted you so that you could accomplish that very goal. God also made you excellent. He made you excellent at accomplishing that task. You are like a fingerprint. Nobody else can accomplish your task. Oh, they can step into your shoes; but they cannot fill your shoes because you are uniquely created to fulfill a purpose that no one else can. **Your calling exceeds you.**

Your calling was not only here before you, it is greater than you are. Your dream is bigger than you are! Well, if it is greater than you are, how are you going to accomplish it?

> **Matthew 5:16** *"Let your light shine before men in such a way that they may **see your good works, and glorify your Father who is in heaven.**"*

Now, I do not know about you, but when *"I"* do a good job, *"I"* get the glory. What about you? When you do a good job, doesn't somebody pat you on the back and say, *"Good job."* How is it, then, that God gets the glory from our good works in this Scripture? It is not natural for somebody to see *"me"* do something well and then turn and give God the glory. The natural response is to give me the glory. There is only one explanation for this. It must be that what I did exceeds my ability to do it. What I did exceeds what I can do humanly. Have you ever come across somebody where you said, *"Wow, Man! That person was just something to be around, God was in them."* Do you know why? They exceeded their human ability to do.

Did you know that God called you to walk in excess of your own ability? When you allow Christ to be formed in you, the work you do so exceeds your own ability that He gets the glory. Your dream is bigger than you are! It is important to understand this because if you do not understand the process that God takes you through you are going to think your dream is too big for you and you are going to give up on it.

So many times people have given up on their dreams because they think it is excessively big for them to do. Your dreams just lie there waiting for you to grab a hold of them. You cannot do it by yourself though. You need your brothers and sisters in Christ. You need God. Without the Holy Spirit operating in your life, you are not going to get there. By understanding your own weaknesses and human inability, you have just empowered God to make something out of you that you could not make out of yourself.

Romans 11:29 for the gifts and the calling of God are irrevocable.

For those of you who do not know what *"irrevocable"* is, it means *"it cannot be given and then taken back."* So let us make this clear in our minds and hearts.

- God called you before you were created.
- He gifted you as you were created to fulfill the call that He already prepared beforehand.
- That means that you are called for life.

Can God make a mistake? God cannot make a mistake! That means that when He called you and gifted you, it was for life no matter if you walked in it or not. He will not take it back because if He took it back He would be saying, *"Oops! I messed up; they cannot do that. I should never have made them that way."* God does not, will not, and cannot mess up, but we do.

I am going to get into that because there are things that keep us from trying to walk in the purpose that God wants us to walk. There are things that can hinder and even stop us. The number one thing that stops Christians from entering into their call is ignorance. You cannot be disqualified from your call simply because you did not know about it. You do know about it. You may not be able to define it, but you know deep inside your spirit that you are here for a reason. That intuitive knowledge is enough to get you to at least start searching.

The next thing that usually stops people is sin. You cannot be disqualified from your call because of sin. If God called me to be a doctor and I am a mechanic, that's not God's fault. If God called me to be a minister and I work in a factory, that's not God's fault. In order to get a hold of what God has called you to do; you have to surrender to the call. If you do not surrender to the call, it will not happen. You have to say, *"Yes, Lord. Make me into the man or woman you have created me to be."*

Women should not take this lightly either. The power of your ability and ministry does not diminish one bit in the eyes of God because of your gender. You have just as much to offer. I want you to understand that God has called you, He loves you, and you are a part of His plan. He is a part of who you are. You have a spirit and the God who is Spirit created it.

> **Romans 7:4** *Therefore, my brethren, you also were made to die to the Law through the body of Christ, so that you might be joined to another, to Him who was raised from the dead,* **in order that we might bear fruit for God.**

Do you see what that verse is saying? I do not know how many people I have dealt with as a minister, as a pastor that said, *"God cannot use me. I am too dirty. I've done too much wrong."* Well, according to what I just read, you became free from the law through the Body of Christ and this happened so that you might be used in service unto God. When you believe in Christ, that He died for you to overcome the deficiencies that you have; that is, I cannot live the Law, you are set free to be used of God. I cannot live perfectly according to God's Law. I failed. You failed. We all failed. Because of that, God had to do something to eliminate that problem so that we can be used in service unto God. He took sin out of the way.

Does that mean we quit sinning completely when we become a Christian? No, as long as you have that flesh suit on, you are going to have trouble with sin. That is just all there is to it. Every one of you has weaknesses and so do I. You will never overcome all of them in this life; at least not until this body is changed and puts on incorruption. Presently, it is a corruptible body; it decays because sin dwells in it.

Read chapter seven of Romans. Sin dwells in our bodies, but it does not disqualify me from the work God has given me to do. Lacking repentance will disqualify me for the moment. However, as long as I see sin as utterly sinful and I am repenting of my failures, I am positioned to bring the Kingdom of God to this earth.

I get rather irritated at some in the Body of Christ that are always trying to disqualify people based upon a moral failure even after that person has repented and turned their lives back to God. Those of you that might be reading this and are of that mindset, are you ready to rip out a major portion of your Bibles? Did you know that major portions of your Bibles were written by murderers! King David was a murderer! Apostle Paul was a murderer! Moses was a murderer!

Let us look at some examples: King David was called to be the king of a nation and was anointed by the prophet of God to be king. Another man was also anointed by the prophet of God to be king before David. King Saul was anointed first and had possession of the throne.

You probably know the story of what happened to Saul. Saul was unwilling to follow the instructions of God and was unrepentant. There is the stark difference between Saul and David. **Sin cannot stop me as long as I am willing to recognize it as sin** and say, *"God, I repent. I know what I did was wrong. I turn from it and follow You."* I have to keep turning away from my sin. I have to keep repenting. Saul did not carry out the instructions of God. God told him to do something specific and he did not carry it out. Even so, it was not that for which he was rejected from being king. He was rejected because he would not repent.

What does this say about you and me when we are unwilling to carry out the call of God upon our lives? The reason Saul did not carry out God's instructions is that he had a wrong view of who he was. He had not come to the place where he placed all of his trust in God to accomplish the call upon his life. He was little in his own eyes. He did not see the potential of God in him to accomplish the call upon his life.

Now look at David. God anointed David to take Saul's place as king of Israel. One day, after David had taken the throne, he was walking upon the roof of his palace and saw a woman taking a bath. Being the king, he can get anything he wants, and he does. Does that not sound a little more sinful to you than what Saul did? Oh, it gets much worse.

David took another man's wife and now she is pregnant. She happens to be married to one of the officers in King David's army. David, like many of us, tried to hide his sin. He called for the officer who is the husband of Bathsheba to return home from the field of battle. David figured that if he brings this fellow home, because he has been away from home for so long, he will have relations with his wife and her pregnancy will look as if the child belongs to her husband rather than to another.

It did not turn out that way, however. The man did not go in unto his wife and he was sent back to the battlefield. David did something unthinkable of someone anointed and positioned by

God. He wrote a letter and he sealed it with the king's seal. He gave it to Bathsheba's husband to take to the captain of the army. The letter told the captain of the army to put Uriah, Bathsheba's husband, on the front lines. Then he was to get into a battle and when the fighting got fierce, withdraw. This would leave Uriah exposed so that he would be killed in battle. David murdered the woman's husband. Not only that, but he murdered others as well in that battle. There were many husbands that would not be coming home to their families because David had them murdered just to hide his sin and get rid of Bathsheba's husband.

Do you think he should be disqualified as king yet? You and I would think so. Nevertheless, what does God say? God sent a prophet to David, exposed his sin, and the first thing David said was, *"I have sinned."* He repented and God did not take him from the throne. In fact, the Bible says God established his throne. If we were left to judge this situation, we would be calling for David to step down and resign his position as king! We must understand that God's calling is irrevocable.

What is the difference between Saul and David? One word—repentance. They both had weaknesses. One of them repented and the other did not. Repentance means that you are going to change your mind about it. It means you recognize what you just did is wrong. It means that you do not try to justify your sin. It means that you do not try to make excuses. Trust me; we know how to make excuses, right?

Our father Adam taught us how to make excuses. The first thing he said when confronted with his sin was, *"God, that woman you sent me... That woman you gave me..."* He started blaming it on her. He started making excuses. God does not want us to make excuses.

We should just stand there and say, *"This is who I am. I am weak. I have a problem in this area. God deliver me. I recognize it as sin."* Then keep walking. Keep walking forward and let God deliver you. That is the whole point. You cannot deliver yourself. You cannot bring yourself out of sin. Only God can do it. You have to say, *"God, I give You the right and the permission to take this out of me. In the meantime, I recognize it as sin. I do not justify it. And I am asking for Your help."* Then every time you commit that sin again, you do the same thing. You turn from it.

People like to blame sin on the devil. Let me clear that up right now. The devil did not make you do it. You have sin in your flesh as I do. You are tempted. You are weak in some areas. That is a fact and the sooner we understand that fact, two things can happen.

Number one: our relationship with God can grow because now we are **not** doing like Adam and Eve by trying to hide from God because we are dirty. In reality, you are not dirty if you have made Jesus your Lord. Jesus said to His apostles, *"You are already clean because of the Word I spoke to you."*

By faith, you are made clean. By faith, you are washed from sin. It is by faith that you can stand before a holy God. It is not your righteousness. It is God's righteousness applied to you so that you can stand before the throne of God. You are clean because of faith. You are clean because you believe.

Imagine if you will, a CEO of a major corporation that has children. Because of his position, people are trying to get in to see him all the time. Because the CEO cannot just see every person that wants audience with him, he has people that are there to filter those important enough to be allowed in and to rebuff those that do not belong there. If one of his children comes to see him, however, they can walk right past the people that are there to buffer him from the public. Why? Because they are his children and everybody knows they must allow them to go in to see their father.

When you believe, the Bible says that God gave you the power to become the sons and daughters of God. That means you have the right to enter boldly into the throne room to see your Daddy. You do not have to feel ashamed to walk in there because the blood of Christ took your shame away. It is not by anything good that you have done, but the good that Jesus did on your behalf. If you try to stand by your own merits, you are doomed. However, if you stand by the merits of Christ in you, you will live.

Secondly, you cannot be disqualified because of weakness or incapability. This should not be confused with the discipline of God. If I am an unrepentant Christian immersed into a sinful life style, I will not approach God because of my relationship with Him because I know that as my Father, He will discipline me as His own child.

> *I Corinthians 1:26 For consider your calling, brethren, that there were not many wise according to the flesh, not many mighty, not many noble;*

So many times in ministry training, we see a very intelligent young man or woman coming through the ranks and we all make the mistake and say, *"Wow! They are going to succeed. They're going to exceed all the rest."* We are looking with the eyes of flesh. We have not seen what God sees. On the other hand, we will see someone struggling in school and having a problem with the work, and with the flesh we will say, *"Oh boy! I don't know if they're going to make it."* It seems though that God proves us wrong every time, and the one that is struggling is the one that God raises up to having a mighty ministry.

One reason that I think this happens is because those with the most talent often rely upon their own talent and those that have the least talent learn early on to rely upon God's power and ability in them. If they have charisma, they rely on their own charisma. If they have great learning skills, they rely upon those. You have to rely on the Holy Spirit. God alone can get you there whether you are intelligent or not.

God will get you there because He called you. He has specifically gifted you that you might get to that place. You do not have anything that can stop you except yourself. Choosing not to go toward your purpose and choosing not to repent will stop you.

> **Romans 8:30** *and these whom He predestined, He also called; and these whom He called, He also justified; and these whom He justified, He also glorified.*

Let us break this down a little bit. **Predestined is not predetermined**. Let me explain the difference. If I have a child and I predestine my own child to become a doctor, that is my destiny for my child. My child could grow up and actually become a mechanic. He may not walk in the destiny for which I have prepared him. Why is it that when I destine my own child to become something, they go in a different direction? The answer can only be that my child is an autonomous human being with the free will to choose their own path no matter how much I prepare them for a particular path.

The idea is this, has God called you? Has He put a destiny within you? Has He predestined you? If He has, then it is up to you to walk that destiny to completion. God is not going to force me to be what I choose not to be. He being God and the Creator of every spirit has predestined every human being to do something and to be something. The Bible says God is not willing that any should perish. The reality, however, is that they do perish. That means that we can disobey God. Everybody is predestined, but when you actually start walking in your destiny, look what happens: Those who are predestined He also called. Those whom He called, He also justified.

What does it mean to be justified? We hear this word often as it relates to sin. We talk about justifying sin. The word means, *"to be made right by acquittal."* In the context of destiny and calling, **it means to be made worthy of your calling.** God called you for something. He made you worthy of it. Do not think that you can skirt your calling because you are unworthy of it. He makes you worthy!

> **John 15:3** *"You are already clean because of the word which I have spoken to you.*

That is what Jesus said. You are already clean. How is it that we disqualify others and ourselves because we feel like we are not clean? It is because you do not understand the grace of God. If you understood the grace of God, you would understand that, *"Yes, I'm a sinner, but I'm also righteous by the blood of Jesus."* How can that be? How can it be that I am a sinner and I am righteous? In myself, in my body, I am a sinner, but because I believe in Jesus, I am made to be righteous.

You believed in Christ and He honors your belief with washing you from all unrighteousness. Now if you will understand that and begin walking into your calling and destiny, you will realize that you can actually be what God created you to be. There are multitudes of Christians that never walked into their destiny because they thought too little of the cross of Christ! They thought that they were too dirty, too untalented, too stupid, too far away, too old, too young, or too weak to fulfill their callings. As a result, they went to the grave with all of the gifting and talents bestowed upon them by God to fulfill His will, taking with them the great treasure that was in them to that grave.

That is why I want to encourage you to tap into what God has created you to be. When you do, you are going to find that which you have been looking for your whole life. You are going to say, *"I am so satisfied doing this."* The reason you are so satisfied doing it is that you are the best at doing your calling because God created you to be the best.

Let me back up a little bit for clarity. Imagine if you will that God created a screwdriver. What would it look like? Would that screwdriver be perfect? Yes, of course it would be perfect. The screwdriver would be perfect and it would work perfectly for the job it was created to do. Therefore, if God created you, what does that mean? He created you perfectly to do the job that you were created for. I want you to understand that word *"perfect."* It is *"teleios"* in the Greek and it means to be *"functionally perfect."*

It does not mean you do not make mistakes. It does not mean you do not have times of faltering. It does not mean you do not fall down. It means you can do what God has created you to do even with the weaknesses you know you have.

In fact, I have screwdrivers in my toolbox that have bent shanks, they have paint on them, and they have nicks in the handle. Yet, with all of the imperfections, they still function perfectly like a screwdriver. They still can take a screw out perfectly and put it back in perfectly because it is *"functionally"* perfect. You too may have scars on the outside, you may have wounds on the inside; but God created you to function perfectly according to the call He gave you. Hallelujah! You can do it because He has already created you to do it.

Your calling is unique to you alone. God has called one person in this manner and another in that. He gave you a perfect niche. We hear people say, *"They found their niche"* to describe someone who has found a work that suits them the best. I love language because often times a saying is actually more accurate than we realize.

If you look at the etymology of the word *"niche"*, you will find that it is from the Latin for *"nest."* A nest is where one belongs. If a bird tries to land in another bird's nest, there is going to be a fight. It carries the meaning that if you are in your nest, you are where you belong because you are great at being in your nest. Because you are in your nest, all others are to get their own nest and quit trying to steal yours from you!

Beware of the dream stealers! Who stole your dream from you? There are people that are not happy because they are not doing what God called them to do. It seems that their unhappiness drives them to make it their life's mission to steal other people's dreams. Because they see themselves as failures, they want to make others fail to justify their failures.

You have to protect your nest; you have to protect your dream. There will be enemies that seek to steal it from you. If you will remain surrendered and repentant I want you to know that no one can take your dream from you! It belongs to you alone! No one else can steal it because you are the only one equipped to fulfill your destiny!

Timelines

I would like you to consider something. When we begin our Christian walk there is a timeline that we start out on. If we submit ourselves to the Lord and to what He has called us to do, then we are walking toward our destiny. However, in reality most of us have not done that. Most of us get off that timeline and start doing our own thing. We start walking our own way and as a result, we create our own timeline. We begin wasting the time that God allotted to us to complete our calling. Then when God disciplines us we realize, *"Man, I'm unhappy over here. Things are not going well. I need to get back to what God called me to."* We walk back over to God's purpose for our existence and get back on that Godly timeline again.

The problem is some time has passed. I have squandered that section of time. I have literally lost opportunities because of my own pride, selfishness, and foolishness. I want you to understand the importance of your life. Did you know that there are people on your timeline where you have to be at a certain place, at a certain time, and with the right message in order to either set their destiny in motion or be a missing piece to their destiny? If you are not there, they are not going to get the help they need.

God has already arranged divine appointments between you and other human beings. He has created you to be there at the right time so that you could hold this person up and maybe even see them saved. How many opportunities have I already missed because of my own disobedience? How many have you missed?

Rejection

What happens if you reject your calling? What happens if you say, *"I don't want to do it? I want to walk my own way."* First, the people that you were destined to impact are going to get to those intersections of time and you will not be there. Yes, there is a burden that comes with our calling. We cannot just pretend it does not exist, walk a different path, and imagine that it is going to be ok. That God will send someone else across his or her path is really not an option if you were uniquely qualified to impact that life.

> *Ephesians 5:6-16 Let no one deceive you with empty words, for because of these things the wrath of God comes upon the sons of disobedience. Therefore do not be partakers with them; for you were formerly darkness, but now you are Light in the Lord; walk as children of Light (for the fruit of the Light consists in all goodness and righteousness and truth), trying to learn what is pleasing to the Lord. Do not participate in the unfruitful deeds of darkness, but instead even expose them; for it is disgraceful even to speak of the things which are done by them in secret. But all things become visible when they are exposed by the light, for everything that becomes visible is light. For this reason it says, "Awake, sleeper, And arise from the dead, And Christ will shine on you." Therefore be careful how you walk, not as unwise men but as wise, (redeeming) making the most of your time, because the days are evil.*

The Greek word for *"redeem"* is a compound word. It means *"from"* and *"marketplace."* The idea of this word is to *"purchase something out of the marketplace."* You are redeemed. That means that you were bought out of the marketplace. You might be thinking, *"I wasn't for sale in a market."* You were in the marketplace. You were a slave and you were bought out of slavery into freedom. Jesus bought you with His blood. The Bible says that you were bought with a price.

Interestingly, we also are given the ability to redeem time that was lost. I want you to get a thorough understanding of this. If Joe Citizen is walking in darkness and God uses me to bring light to him to the end that he is saved; I have bought time by setting this man on his timeline. This man will now be able to intersect with heaven and begin walking toward his destiny and in this, I was able to redeem time that I had lost! That is why we cannot look at how old we are to decide if we will start walking out our purpose. It is never too late to start purchasing time from the marketplace of darkness.

> **Colossians 4:5** *Conduct yourselves with wisdom toward outsiders, (redeeming the time) making the most of the opportunity. (emphasis is mine)*

The Greek reads literally, *"In wisdom walk around to the ones outside, the season buying out."* I have seen too many people give up because they think they have exhausted their time. They look at their lives and are so reproached by their own conduct that they refuse to enter in and begin redeeming the time. They could do so much with so little time because the ones they rescue would allow them to continue working long after they are deceased. If you are reading this and have not thought to begin your destiny because you think it is too late; redeem the time by walking into your destiny.

Everything God has called you to do, even though it might seem insignificant to you now, has great import in the hands of

God. You might think it is unimportant, however, you do not see the grand scheme. You do not see the orchestration of your God. When you think about it, He gets so much out of every little thing we do. When you go through the checkout line and you smile at the checkout person, and treat them with kindness and respect, you may have changed their life. That person may have thought, *"I am sick of this life. No one loves me. No one likes me. I think I will end it today. It's over."* Nevertheless, because you treated them nicely, you gave them a reason to keep going.

Before you were saved, the devil was actively hiding the good news of Jesus so that you would not become a child of God. Once you became a child of God, the devil shifted his tactics. Now he is going to fight you in order to stop you from doing the work God called you to do. He is going to make you feel condemned and guilty with sin. He is going to try to make you think that you are inadequate, that you are unable, that you are not good enough, that you are not strong enough, and that you are not smart enough. He is going to say to you, *"You can't do it."* I have a message for you! Your dream might be bigger than you, but so is your God! He is bigger than you are and He is the One Who gave you the dream. All things are possible to them that believe! You can ignore your calling and leave it unfulfilled; **but**—oh, that *"but"* is a big one— it is devastating. You can go your own way, but it is destructive.

Examples of Loss

Judas provides for us an example regarding the rejecting of one's call. Everybody knows who Judas is. Judas was the one that betrayed Jesus. What is interesting is that because Judas betrayed Christ, most think that betrayal was actually his purpose and destiny. When we look at the life of Judas and Jesus interacting with him we see a story unfold that reveals a profound truth. In this story, we can all see a time in our own lives where we were rebellious and we sought to do our own things rather than to die to Christ.

In order to understand this story there are some things that need to be understood. The first thing that you must understand is that Jesus is not just a human, but He is also God. He is God incarnate, God in the flesh. Because Jesus is God and it is said of God that He cannot lie, we are left with the knowledge that it is impossible for Jesus to lie or deceive in any way. With that knowledge, we need to look at what Jesus said to Judas.

The Bible says that he called twelve men whom He also named apostles. An apostle is a calling, a destiny. That means when Jesus called Judas an apostle, being an apostle was his destiny. Jesus knew he would also betray him, yet that does not release Judas of the burden to fulfill his destiny. If we take this at face value, we can conclude that it was not the destiny of Judas to betray Christ. Temptation had conceived and brought forth sin and Judas betrayed his Mentor, Jesus.

In fact, you will remember that Judas was sitting at the last supper with the other disciples and Jesus when Jesus said, *"Go and do what Satan has put in your heart."* Judas was not following the words that he had heard Jesus preach in the synagogue; he was not following the command of his Mentor who had invited him to follow Him. No, instead, Judas made the decision to hear another voice; he was following the words of the enemy. Jesus had called him an apostle, but Satan had given him a different report. Judas, by listening to the devil, was deceived in his heart.

For Judas, the story had a tragic ending. Judas committed suicide after realizing what he had done. That left the group of disciples short one person to fulfill the mandate their Mentor had given them when he revealed their ultimate destiny of judging the twelve tribes of Israel. We pick up the narrative in Acts where we now have just eleven men and the twelfth spot has to be filled.

> *Acts 1:15-17 At this time Peter stood up in the midst of the brethren (a gathering of about one hundred and twenty persons was there together), and said, "Brethren, the Scripture had to be fulfilled, which the Holy Spirit foretold by the mouth of David concerning Judas, who became a guide to those who arrested Jesus. For he was counted among us and received his share in this ministry.*

Because of the wording of that section of Scripture, many have concluded that Judas was destined to be the betrayer. However, if you will look closely, the other apostles recognized that Judas had a share or part in ministry. This was not given by anyone else, but Jesus, their Mentor. Jesus is the one who gives the ministry to a person according to the twelfth chapter of First Corinthians. Again, Jesus cannot lie being God in the flesh. The foretelling of Judas' deeds did not predetermine them. Judas is still completely responsible for his actions and his refusal to fulfill his destiny.

> *Acts 1:18-20 (Now this man acquired a field with the price of his wickedness, and falling headlong, he burst open in the middle and all his intestines gushed out. And it became known to all who were living in Jerusalem; so that in their own language that field was called Hakeldama, that is, Field of Blood.) "For it is written in the book of Psalms, 'Let his homestead be made desolate, And let no one dwell in it'; and, **'Let another man take his office.'***

Judas was called to be one of the premium apostles. He was to be known as one of the twelve. God's foreknowledge revealed the decisions Judas would make before Judas ever existed. This did not force Judas to make those decisions, rather it only revealed them. If I make the decision to buy a Ford truck tomorrow, God already knew my decision and could have written it in advance. Let us not, therefore, think for one second that Judas was forced or destined to be a betrayer of the Christ.

God says; let someone else take his office. Office bespeaks of placement by God into a destiny that Judas was formed to fulfill. What an honor to be chosen by God to be one of the Disciples of the Great God to judge one of the twelve tribes of Israel. I have to ask, what writing of this apostle do we not have because he was more interested in following his own ways rather than God's ways? Do you know the name of that apostle who replaced Judas? Not many people do. Do you know why? It is because Judas was uniquely created to do that job better than any other human being, and he walked away from it.

Yes, somebody else took his place, but he could not fill his shoes. That man who took Judas' place was named Matthias. Interestingly, you never hear from him again for the rest of the Scriptures. Ponder that for a moment. Only you can do what God has called you to do. Other people can try to take up your work, but they cannot do it like you because you were uniquely created to do it. You were like a fingerprint that is so different from any other and only your life was unable to unlock the destiny given to you.

Another example of callings unfulfilled is this time a city. God not only calls individuals, but He calls cities and nations to accomplish His work. The city I speak of is Jerusalem.

Lamentations 1:8-9 *Jerusalem sinned greatly,*
Therefore she has become an unclean thing. All
who honored her despise her because they have
seen her nakedness; even she herself groans and
*turns away. Her uncleanness was in her skirts; **she***
did not consider her future. Therefore she has
***fallen astonishingly**; she has no comforter. "See, O*
Lord, my affliction, For the enemy has magnified
himself!"

If we do not consider our destiny, if we do not consider that which God has called us for, our ruin will be awesome. We can do some things; we can live life, but we are not going to have satisfaction until we live it the way God created us to live it. I am not talking about sin verses righteousness. I am talking about walking into the calling for which God created you. If you run away from it, there are grave consequences.

We know another man that ran away from his calling. His name was Jonah. Do you remember how his destruction was awesome? Do you remember how the great fish swallowed him? Jesus even pointed back to Jonah and said this, *"Just as Jonah was in the belly of the fish three days and three nights, so the Son of Man will be in the belly of the earth three days and three nights."* Some people say that Jonah literally died and was resurrected when he was spit up on the beach. How many know something like that will make you walk into your calling?

The point I am trying to make is that we have to find that which God called us to do, get equipped and discipled, and walk in it. If you do not, like Jerusalem, your calling can destroy you because you ignored it and because you did not consider your future. I do not know how many people we have counseled that have walked away from what God called them to do. The result is that their life is in utter ruin.

> *I Corinthians 3:11-15 For no man can lay a foundation other than the one which is laid, which is Jesus Christ. Now if any man builds on the foundation with gold, silver, precious stones, wood, hay, straw, each man's work will become evident; for the day will show it because it is to be revealed with fire, and the fire itself will test the quality of each man's work. If any man's work which he has built on it remains, he will receive a reward. If any man's work is burned up, he will suffer loss; but he himself will be saved, yet so as through fire.*

What is interesting about this section of Scripture is that the Christian faces a much different judgment than the unbeliever. The unbeliever has to give an account for their sin and their denial of the only sacrifice that is able to save them. The Christian, on the other hand, has to give an account about their destiny and calling. The primary fear of God in the unbeliever's life should be in regard to sin. The primary fear of God in the believer's life should be regarding accomplishing or finishing one's calling. I reveal this because I would like to see Christians start looking at their godly potential and the fulfillment of calling in a more serious light.

Anything I do of myself is wood, hay, and stubble. Those are the things that will be burned up when I stand before God. I do not want anyone to be confused. This has nothing to do with salvation. You are already saved as a believer. However, you are going to stand before the judgment seat of Christ to give an account for what you have done with your saved life.

The quality of a person's work is found in truth. That is, to the degree that you walk in truth, in the reality of your existence, in the reality of God's Word, and in the reality of being created in God's image, you will bear fruit that will result in reward. On the other hand, if you choose to walk in deception that states that what you think is important for your life takes precedence, then you will find your works being burned up. Yet, even if every work is burned up, you still have salvation. Even so, you will stand shamefully before the Son of God who gave Himself to you so that you could be free to do what He created you to do.

Jesus said, *"Why do you call me Lord, and do not do the things I say?"* Think about that. If I called you master and yet I never did anything you told me to do, the title is pretty much lip service, is it not? You must understand that the fulfillment of your calling requires your participation.

> *Ephesians 4:1* *Therefore I, the prisoner of the Lord,*
> *implore you to walk in a manner worthy of the*
> *calling with which you have been called,*

What does it mean to walk in a manner worthy of the calling to which we are called? Is it to walk sinless before God? Can it mean that? We can find that answer by looking at the word *"worthy"* in the Greek. The phrase *"manner worthy of"* is a single Greek word that means to be *"of equal weight."* Walking in a manner worthy of your call is to give somber consideration to the weight of what God has called you to do.

It means that Paul is calling us to put weight and importance on all of our decisions in equal value to the call. That means that I will look at my calling in the weight of the fact that God is the One who has called me and He deserves my unconditional surrender to

His purpose and calling. What a fitting way to open the chapter that reveals the fivefold ministry to the Church.

It is also vital for you to understand that you need your brothers and sisters and you need the ministry to help define those things that God has called you to do. The prophetic ministry is awesome in that endeavor. The **prophetic ministry** can see the calling in you.

The **teaching ministry** and the **apostolic ministry** can bring those things out of you and start preparing and equipping you. The **pastoral ministry** can protect you through the process. The **evangelistic ministry** can get you to that point where you are willing to start the process of discipleship. We need each other. We need all the callings. Moreover, when we work hand in hand, shoulder to shoulder, we are empowered to succeed.

> *Hebrews 11:8 By faith Abraham, when he was called, obeyed by going out to a place which he was to receive for an inheritance; and he went out, not knowing where he was going.*

Abraham is called the father of our faith. Never has there been a man that more expressed extreme feats of faith than Abraham did. Now, I want you to think of this; here is a person, he is comfortable. He has his own place, his own family, and things are going great. He lives in a big city. The economy is good. He has a job. God shows up and said to him, *"Abram, leave everything and go to a place that I will show you."*

He actually says okay. Most of us would be bargaining with God or blaming the devil. God did not tell him where he was going, only to prepare to go. God told him not to take his family with him. He could only take his wife and servants. When

Abraham left, he did take some family. He took with him his father and his cousin, Lot. It seems as if he is feeling a little unsure about this call.

When we first hear that we are called many of us are a bit unsure as well. We cling to those things that we think give us security. Abraham clings to his family by taking them with him when God had instructed him not to. Did God reject Abraham because he was unsure of things? Not at all. God worked with Abraham where he was at in his faith.

Nevertheless, there was consequence to be felt by not adhering to God's instructions. Abraham's father died when they got to the first city. God will begin removing anything that we find security in other than God Himself. Abraham learned many lessons in trusting God along the way. He trusted God to protect him and his wife Sarah, and to fulfill His promise of giving them a son. Ultimately, Abraham trusted God for the life of that son even though God had asked him to offer his son as a sacrifice. In that last act of faith, Abraham sealed for all time any doubt concerning his faith and resolve to follow God to his destiny.

> ***Philippians 3:8-9*** *More than that, I count all things to be loss in view of the surpassing value of knowing Christ Jesus my Lord, for whom I have suffered the loss of all things, and count them but rubbish so that I may gain Christ, and may be found in Him, not having a righteousness of my own derived from the Law, but that which is through faith in Christ, the righteousness which comes from God on the basis of faith,*

Paul was able to verbalize succinctly what it means to answer the call of God upon your life. Paul counted all things to be loss.

Everything of value suddenly changes when the man or woman comes face to face with Jesus through faith. Suddenly they see what is valuable and what is fluff. The next item that Paul reveals is the importance of grace in answering the call. If we do not have a handle on the grace of God, we are tempted to enter into our own works. Any time we rely upon ourselves, we will fall.

> ***Philippians 3:10-12*** *that I may know Him and the power of His resurrection and the fellowship of His sufferings, being conformed to His death; in order that I may attain to the resurrection from the dead. Not that I have already obtained it or have already become perfect, but I press on so that I may lay hold of that for which also I was laid hold of by Christ Jesus.*

Apostle Paul said I am not perfect; I have not attained perfection. Nevertheless, I am pressing on. I am pressing on. I am pressing on. I am going forward. Nothing is going to impede me. I am going to keep going forward. I am going to lay hold of that for which God laid hold of me. You have to do that. God has a purpose for laying hold of us and He invites us to lay hold of that purpose just as He laid hold of our life.

> ***Philippians 3:13-14*** *Brethren, I do not regard myself as having laid hold of it yet; but one thing I do: forgetting what lies behind and reaching forward to what lies ahead, I press on toward the goal for the prize of the upward call of God in Christ Jesus.*

Do not let your past come up and speak to you. Your past is your past is your past. Repent of your past and go forward. We can learn from our past, but we should not let our past torment us. We have to walk forward. God came to me one day and He said this to my spirit, *"Son, every moment you spend thinking about past failures, you are spending losing today's battles."*

The only way you can win today's battles is to quit fighting yesterday's battles and engage today's troubles. The only way to go forward is to press ahead and forget what is behind you. If you are constantly looking back, you are going to run into a tree. You have to focus on where you are going and that is what Paul is saying. *"I've not apprehended this yet, but I'm focused. I'm pressing forward to that which God called me to."* Forgetting those things that are behind and reaching forward to those things that are ahead.

Paul knew about what he was talking. He understood it. If you put all of Paul's writings in chronological order, you will see humility develop in Paul's life where he goes from saying, *"Hey! I am just as good as one of the twelve."* Then chronologically, you get a little later in life and he says, *"They are the supreme apostles. I'm just an apostle."* Then he gets a little further down in time and he says, *"I'm not even worthy to be called an apostle."* Finally, in the last letter he wrote, he said, *"This is a true and faithful saying. That Jesus Christ came to save sinners of whom I am chief."* Even so, notice that Paul did not give up on his call. He kept going forward. He did not let sin stop him. He said, *"I'm the chief of sinners."* but he did not stop.

How many times has the devil whispered to you after you have had a failure and said, *"You're not worthy to do what God's called you to do. Give it up. You are not worthy. You do not have what it takes. You've got to clean yourself up first."* That will never happen. No person that says, *"I've got to clean myself up first"* understands how the grace of God works. Nor do they ever clean themselves up.

The grace of God tells us that He, Christ has to clean us up. We are incapable of cleaning our selves. It takes faith in Christ; in the blood of Jesus to be cleaned. You have to keep going forward. Your dream is bigger than you. You cannot do it without Him.

Your dream will also bring glory to God because He gives you His ability. Apostle Paul said, *"God, Your strength is perfected in my weakness. So, I will boast in my weakness, that I might have more of the power of God."* I need the power of God in my life so I am going to boast in my weaknesses. You have just as much opportunity to become what God called you to as the next person does. You are going to fall down. The devil will trick you and you will fall. You will be weak in your flesh and you will fail but you have to keep getting up.

Do not let your failures hold you down. Keep getting up. Recognize what you did. Do not justify it, but keep getting up. The righteous man, the Bible says, falls seven times and gets up. Think about that. It is not about falling, it is about getting up. We need to be people that are marked by our tenacity of purpose through the manifestation of getting up when we fall.

Job was called the most righteous man in the earth. God gave a description of Job in which He described the qualities that made him the most righteous man in the earth. One of those qualities was that he was always turning away from sin. Always turning away from sin is not saying that he did not sin. Rather that was a perfect description of what true repentance is. It is turning away from the sins you have committed. Acknowledging that God and His laws are right and they are the standard from which we measure our own behavior.

The reason we know that God was not saying that Job did not sin is by looking at Job's life. When you read about Job, you find that he sacrificed every day. Why? It is because Job knew that he was a sinner. He knew that he had weaknesses, but he was turning away from them. He was not trying to give an excuse for his sin. He was coming into agreement with God that it was sin and that he needed a sacrifice to cover that sin. The fact that he was sacrificing lambs on the altar proved that he did not agree with his own sin.

The fact that you believe in Jesus Christ and you apply His blood to your life proves that you do not agree with your sin. So stand up! Go forward! Enter into that call that God has created just for you. Take the clarion call to *"just do it"* seriously by committing yourself to your destiny right now!

Mentoring

O nce you have committed yourself to your call, there is now the obligation of following God's instructions to actualize destiny. If you think you can achieve your destiny by simply running after it, you have already lost the race. This race, this noble pursuit, can only be won by proper preparation.

Can you imagine a racecar that is not prepared before a race? Can you imagine an athlete that did not train in their sport? God does not just reveal destiny without giving proper instruction for your course. This is where the necessity of discipleship is revealed. Discipleship is not a one-person endeavor. Explicit in the Scriptures is the need to be equipped for the work God has called you to do. Finding that leader with God's help is the next step.

> **Hebrews 13:17** *Obey your leaders and submit to them, for they keep watch over your souls as those who will give an account. Let them do this with joy and not with grief, for this would be unprofitable for you.*

Definition – *Obey*

The Greek word is **peitho**. (pi·tho) and it means, *"to persuade or convince."*

The Hebrew word is **shama**. (shaw·mah) and it means, *"to hear."*

The idea of the word *"obey"* is not what we normally think of the word *"obey."* The Greek gives us the idea that obedience is connected to a reasonable argument that persuades the hearer that the argument is true. Thus, the onus is on the leader to provide that convincing argument from the Scriptures. If the leader is able to do this it will produce faith, which in turn should produce the obedience.

The Hebrew has the idea of hearing and then doing. The Bible says in Romans 10:17, *"So then faith cometh by hearing, and hearing by the Word of God."*

Definition – *Submit*

The Greek word is **hupeiko** (hoop·i·ko) and it means, *"to yield or retire."*

The idea then is for the disciple to be convinced by hearing a reasonable argument from the Scriptures and act upon it. Then, when the person is convinced of the leader's ability to handle the Word of God, they should submit themselves to the leader. To submit one's self means to withdraw. The idea is that one steps back and allows another to lead.

The Role of the Disciple

The disciple must understand that they are invited to witness the life of the leader so that they too can build lives of integrity and understanding. The disciple's role in this relationship is to be submissive but **not at the expense of free will**. It is a decision by the disciple to sit under a person who is willing to pour into his or her life.

It is important there is agreement between disciple and leader so that there will be little dissension. If the disciple will understand that his position is subservient and that position is only achieved by an act of his free will and **not by compulsion**, then the relationship can flourish. Where in the gospel is it evident that Jesus **demanded** that His disciples follow Him? Even though He said, *"follow Me,"* they had to be willing to do so. It was an invitation that could have been rejected or accepted.

Mentoring is supposed to mature individuals to the place where THEY can begin to make disciples, to the end that the very truth given by Jesus to His disciples that was guarded and transferred to us from other men of God, would continue to be passed down through generations.

> *John 6:67-70 (GW) So Jesus asked the twelve apostles, "Do you want to leave me, too?" Simon Peter answered Jesus, "Lord, to what person could we go? Your words give eternal life. Besides, we believe and know that you are the Holy One of God." Jesus replied, "I chose all twelve of you. Yet, one of you is a devil."*

The Role of the Leader

In the government of the Church there is an emphasis placed upon this relationship of the leader to the disciple and the disciple to the leader. It is a close relationship. In modern mega ministries we do not see this kind of relationship possible. It is not possible for one minister to mentor that many people. This is why larger ministries have adopted the cell group theory. It sets leaders over small groups and thus achieves the training they need.

Jesus set the pattern. He took twelve men into His circle. I find it interesting that the business world tells us that a manager can only effectively manage eleven people. Jesus invited twelve men to follow Him and to learn about the kingdom of God so they could communicate that information to the generations that followed them. Is it any wonder then that on the foundational level of the new temple wall there will be twelve stones with the Apostles' names upon them? They constructed the foundation of the building that we call the Church. Now Jesus had many disciples, but they were not mentored like His twelve apostles.

> **Mark 10:42-45** *Calling them to Himself, Jesus said to them, "You know that those who are recognized as rulers of the Gentiles lord it over them; and their great men exercise authority over them. But it is not this way among you, but whoever wishes to become great among you shall be your servant; and whoever wishes to be first among you shall be slave of all. For even the Son of Man did not come to be served, but to serve, and to give His life a ransom for many."*

> **Luke 22:25-28** *And He said to them, "The kings of the Gentiles lord it over them; and those who have authority over them are called 'Benefactors.' But it is not this way with you, but the one who is the greatest among you must become like the youngest, and the leader like the servant. For who is greater, the one who reclines at the table or the one who*

serves? Is it not the one who reclines at the table? But I am among you as the one who serves."

__I Peter 5:1-5 (NCV)__ Now I have something to say to the elders in your group. I also am an elder. I have seen Christ's sufferings, and I will share in the glory that will be shown to us. I beg you to shepherd God's flock, for whom you are responsible. Watch over them because you want to, not because you are forced. That is how God wants it. Do it because you are happy to serve, not because you want money. Do not be like a ruler over people you are responsible for, but be good examples to them. Then when Christ, the Chief Shepherd, comes, you will get a glorious crown that will never lose its beauty. In the same way, younger people should be willing to be under older people. And all of you should be very humble with each other.

__Proverbs 3:34__ "God is against the proud, but he gives grace to the humble."

It should be obviously clear that the leader is not to lord over the flock. Leaders are to be examples to the flock.

The Leader Should be Like a Father

__I Corinthians 4:14-16__ I do not write these things to shame you, but to admonish you as my beloved children. For if you were to have countless tutors in Christ, yet you would not have many fathers, for in Christ Jesus I became your father through the gospel. Therefore I exhort you, be imitators of me.

Being a father to a disciple is a big commitment of time and effort. There is a necessary emotional attachment as well in this relationship, whereas in a tutor to student relationship that same attachment is not of necessity.

This should also show you why in our foundation text that the author said, *"let them do so with joy"* (Hebrews 13:17). That means that a disciple has the power to bring joy or discouragement based upon his level of submission to the leader.

Also, note that Paul said he became their father in Christ Jesus. This is a warm description of Paul's love for his disciples. It is the role of the leader to become a father to the disciple and it is the role of the disciple to become like a son or daughter to the leader.

The Leader Must be a Good Role Model

> *Hebrews 13:7 Remember those who led you, who spoke the word of God to you; and considering the result of their conduct, imitate their faith.*

If the disciple is to imitate the faith of their leaders that would presuppose that the leader had faith to be imitated. The leader must be a man or woman of faith. Understanding that faith is information from God believed to be true and acted upon would give us the indication that the leaders must be skilled and have the ability to rightly use the Word of God.

> *II Timothy 2:15 Be diligent to present yourself approved to God as a workman who does not need*

to be ashamed, accurately handling the word of truth.

The Leader Must be Diligent

*Romans 12:6-8 We have different gifts, according to the grace given us. If a man's gift is prophesying, let him use it in proportion to his faith. If it is serving, let him serve; if it is teaching, let him teach; if it is encouraging, let him encourage; if it is contributing to the needs of others, let him give generously; **if it is leadership, let him govern diligently;** if it is showing mercy, let him do it cheerfully.*

To lead diligently means that the leader will show persistence and hard working effort to accomplish discipleship goals.

The End Result of Mentoring

Ephesians 4:11-16 And He gave some as apostles, and some as prophets, and some as evangelists, and some as pastors and teachers, for the equipping of the saints for the work of service, to the building up of the body of Christ; until we all attain to the unity of the faith, and of the knowledge of the Son of God, to a mature man, to the measure of the stature, which belongs to the fullness of Christ.

As a result, we are no longer to be children, tossed here and there by waves and carried about by every wind of doctrine, by the trickery of men, by craftiness in deceitful scheming; but speaking the truth in love, we are to grow up in all aspects into Him who is the head, even Christ, from whom the whole body, being fitted and held together by what every joint supplies, according to the proper working of each individual part, causes the growth of the body for the building up of itself in love.

To Equip the Saints

It should be noted that the five ministries mentioned in verse eleven are for the equipping of the saints. To equip the saints means to train them and make them ready for ministry.

For the Work of God

The saints are trained or equipped in order to do the work of God. This is something usually placed upon the ministry in our modern culture.

To the Building up of the Body of Christ

The purpose of training is linear. It is so the disciple can begin to do the work of God in order that the Body of Christ is built up. The process of building up the Body of Christ starts with training that will result in increase. Building up the Body is primarily that of edification and maturity so that the whole Body becomes mature.

Till we all Attain the Unity of Faith and of the Knowledge of God

When the Body is trained, it builds up the Body to maturity, which brings us into unity of faith. Unity of faith means that we as a Body come into agreement concerning the doctrines of Christ. Unity in the knowledge of God is basically the same thing. It is believing the same things concerning the doctrines of Christ.

To a Mature Man

Again, training which builds up the Body and brings unity results in maturity.

To the Measure of the Stature Which Belongs to the Fullness of Christ

Each of us is like a measuring vessel. God is the One who sees how full we are with faith. The building up of the Body is measured in the knowledge of God. Knowledge is information believed to be true. The knowledge of God is information believed to be true about God. That is faith.

As we grow our faith through hearing the Word and studying the Word, we are being filled up. Once you are filled up, you are ready to become the one who does the equipping of saints. You go from being a disciple to one who makes disciples.

As a Result, we are no Longer to be Children

Children are marked by certain qualities. Babies are unable to eat meat. Children are not able to conceptualize certain truths and can be rebellious or disobedient. They are also easy to deceive and are unable to sense certain dangers.

No Longer Tossed Here and There by Waves

The Greek word for waves means to be agitated mentally. The things that agitate us mentally are trials. Once trained, we will not be easily moved when the waves of trials come our way.

No Longer Carried About by Every Wind of Doctrine

When we come to the place where we are thoroughly equipped, we will not be easily deceived concerning doctrine. There are those that try to trick, and they use their craftiness to scheme and plan to deceive. When we are thoroughly equipped, we will be founded in sound teaching, and those that try to lead the unlearned astray will be exposed.

Speaking the Truth in Love

Speaking the truth without love makes the truth useless. If there are any other motives other than love, it is the truth that suffers.

Christ the Head

Jesus retains at all times headship over His Church. There will be leaders who think that they have been appointed head, but they are not. Leaders are overseers at most. That is, leaders oversee the operation of the Church, but God is the One Who gives the Church direction and animation.

Being Fitted and Held Together by What Every Joint Supplies

A joint has no mass. It is simply a point where two parts come together. Christ, therefore, fits two parts together, and the combination of talents and gifts that each part supplies holds that joint together. This is what we call a divine relationship. God puts individuals together with others to facilitate the movement of His Body.

According to the Proper Working of Each Individual Part

As long as each part works properly, the joint is held together. When we defer to one another's gifts, we are able to accomplish the will of God on the earth. If we compete and grasp for honor or power, we inhibit the movement of the Body, and we prohibit God's will from being done on the earth.

Review

From this, the Body of Christ will be built up in love! Now go back, re-read this section of verses, and put it all together.

The Proper Relationship to Authority

We cannot conclude this study without mentioning the importance of a correct relationship to authority. The Bible is full of examples on this subject. One only need think for a moment, and the name of Korah comes to mind. Korah, along with 250 leaders, came against the authority of Moses, and the earth opened up and swallowed them and their families. The Word tells us that they went alive into hell. I am not saying this to suggest that the earth will open up and swallow those that rebel against authority; rather, I only want to suggest that God does not look well upon it.

Then we have the opposite side of this scenario. In this story, the one **in authority** is demon possessed. God anoints a successor to this man, however, the successor does not try to usurp the demon-possessed man's position. This is the story of King Saul and King David. Even though David was anointed as king by God's commission to the prophet Samuel, David understands POSITIONAL AUTHORITY, and he refuses to go after the throne even though he is the rightful king. Saul chases David from place to place to try to kill him, but David refuses to harm a single hair of Saul's head even though he has many opportunities. This is a classic example of the **right relationship to authority.**

The following excerpt is taken from the course *"The Life of Faith,"* by Dr. Michael Lake of Biblical Life College and Seminary.

What process should be used when you have a conflict with authority?

> *1. Pray about the situation, and try to get the mind of God.*

> *2. Make sure your attitudes are of a pure motive.*

> *3. Make sure your conscience is clear, that you have corrected your offending attitudes, and that*

you have sought forgiveness and made restitution as
far as possible.

4. Discern the intention of the one over you. Is he
looking out for your well-being? What is his frame
of reference?

5. Then, with that information, design a creative
alternative that satisfies both him and you.

6. Without condemning him, present that alternative
to him as an appeal, emphasizing how it will meet
his goals. Leave the final decision with him.

7. Give God time to change his mind. Know that
God will be putting pressure on the leader, that he,
therefore, will probably put pressure on you, and
that God can use that pressure to build Godly
character in your life. Make sure you constantly
respond in love and righteousness."

Would it be right to go to other leaders and try to expel this authority?

It is not the position of the disciple to remove a leader. Remember that the leader is accountable to God and other leaders, and, if God so desires, He will remove the leader from his position.

III John 9-14 I wrote something to the church; but
Diotrephes, who loves to be first among them, does
not accept what we say. For this reason, if I come, I
will call attention to his deeds which he does,
unjustly accusing us with wicked words; and not

satisfied with this, he himself does not receive the brethren, either, and he forbids those who desire to do so and puts them out of the church.

Beloved, do not imitate what is evil, but what is good. The one who does good is of God; the one who does evil has not seen God. Demetrius has received a good testimony from everyone, and from the truth itself; and we add our testimony, and you know that our testimony is true.

I had many things to write to you, but I am not willing to write them to you with pen and ink; but I hope to see you shortly, and we will speak face to face.

The Challenge

Make it a point to show honor and respect to authority, especially to those that watch over you. Even those that are not in authority over you, but are in a position of authority, should be shown respect and honor by you.

What Role Does Doctrine Play?

Chapter Four

I need to take you back to the reformation in order to bring this subject into perspective. The reformation marked a period of our history that represented a call to truth. The universal church had become structured in such a way that there was no recourse for those who sawthe indulgences taking place to bring complaint and resolution. When it became obvious, men of conviction began separating from the church. This exodus was not a quick one, nor was it stark. God rose up reformer after reformer and this took place over a period of some 300 years.

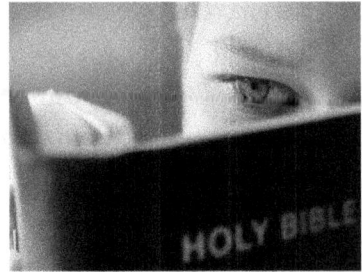

The problem with the reformation is that the Protestants began dividing among themselves. There were basically three lines of division. The cause of these divisions was doctrinal differences. When you open a door of separation, as honorable and right as it may be, there is the danger that division becomes acceptable under lesser conditions. In other words, if it were right to divide from the universal church for reasons of indulgence and doctrine, then it becomes acceptable to divide over a doctrinal issue.

From those three streams, we now have a whole tree of divisions in the Church. When looking back at the divisions that have taken place, and we ask the question, *"What was the defining element that caused division?"* the answer would be – doctrine. The next natural move among the Church then is to get rid of the cause of division.

Today, it is common to turn on the TV and hear a preacher tell us that doctrine is not important. Their argument is that doctrine is what divided the Church. That means that in their minds, doctrine should be avoided because it causes something bad.

Since they see doctrine as something negative, they instead concentrate on those things in the Church that do not divide. Those things are worship, relationship, service to the community, etc. They see worship as a uniting factor and doctrine as a dividing factor. What we need to address then is the biblical position on this.

One thing we need to see within the statement that, *"Doctrine is not important"* is that the statement itself becomes a doctrine and is therefore self-refuted. What we need to ask is, *"How important is doctrine from God's perspective?"*

> *John 7:16-18 So Jesus answered them and said, "My teaching is not Mine, but His who sent Me. "If anyone is willing to do His will, he will know of the teaching, whether it is of God or whether I speak from Myself. "He who speaks from himself seeks his own glory; but He who is seeking the glory of the One who sent Him, He is true, and there is no unrighteousness in Him.*

What is Doctrine?

The word *"doctrine"* is from the Latin *"docere"* which means to **teach**. This is also where we get the word *"doctor"* which means **teacher**. When we look up the term translated *"doctrine"* in the New Testament we find that it means teaching. There is no word translated in the Hebrew as doctrine, but there is for teaching.

Since they are synonymous, we will look at the Hebrew for *"teach."*

Definition - *Teach*

The Greek word is ***did·as·kal·ee·ah*** and it simply means *"teaching."*

The Hebrew word is ***Yaw-Raw***

(1) to cast, Ex. 15:4; e.g. a lot, Josh. 18:6; an arrow, 1 Sa. 20:36, 37; Ps. 11:2; 64:5; Num. 21:30. Part. יוֹרֶה, an archer, 1 Ch. 10:3.
(2) to lay foundations (compare Gr. Βάλλεσθαι ἄστυ, for to lay the foundations of a city; Syr. ܪܡܐ to cast, to place a foundation), to found. Job 38:6, "who laid (or founded, or placed) its corner stone." Gen. 31:51, "behold the pillar אֲשֶׁר יָרִיתִי which I have founded," i.e. placed, or raised.
(3) to sprinkle, to water (pr. to throw water, to scatter drops, compare זָרַק), Hos. 6:3. Hence part. יוֹרֶה the former rain, see above, page 343, B. - (Gesenius, 2003)

Casting or Throwing

The Hebrew gives three basic pictures for the word that means doctrine. The first of these pictures is that of casting or throwing something. This picture comes to full clarity in the parable of the sower. For in this parable we start with a man who casts something. We pick up where Jesus is explaining His parable. This becomes extremely important because Jesus identifies this particular parable as a key in understanding all of His parables.

> **Mark 4:13-20** *And He said to them, "Do you not understand this parable? How will you understand all the parables? "The sower sows the word. These are the ones who are beside the road where the word is sown; and when they hear, immediately Satan comes and takes away the word which has been sown in them. "In a similar way these are the ones on whom seed was sown on the rocky places, who, when they hear the word, immediately receive it with joy; and they have no firm root in themselves, but are only temporary; then, when affliction or persecution arises because of the word, immediately they fall away. "And others are the ones on whom seed was sown among the thorns; these are the ones who have heard the word, but the worries of the world, and the deceitfulness of riches, and the desires for other things enter in and choke the word, and it becomes unfruitful. "And those are the ones on whom seed was sown on the good soil; and they hear the word and accept it and bear fruit, thirty, sixty, and a hundredfold. "*

The seed is the Word of God. The seed has to be sown or cast. If it is not cast or taught, there is nothing to believe; there is no growth, there is no fruit. For fruit to exist there must be at some point seed cast upon the ground. **To say that doctrine is not important is to refuse to cast seed into the ground.**

The bearing of fruit is the work of the person who accepted the seed. Jesus defines fruit as our works. *"By their fruit you shall know them. "* This means when we believe the Word of God being taught, that seed will grow and bear fruit causing our works to display the attributes of the seed sown. After providing an explanation of this parable and revealing to the disciples that it is the key to understanding all of the others, Jesus gives them a slightly different parable.

> *Mark 4:26-29 And He was saying, "The kingdom of God is like a man who casts seed upon the soil; and he goes to bed at night and gets up by day, and the seed sprouts and grows—how, he himself does not know. "The soil produces crops by itself; first the blade, then the head, then the mature grain in the head. "But when the crop permits, he immediately puts in the sickle, because the harvest has come."*

With the key in place, this parable becomes easy to understand. A man cast seed. A man teaches the Word. The condition of the heart determines whether the seed will grow or not. The crop is a result of the partnership between the seed and the soil. Our works are a result of the partnership of the condition of our hearts and the Word of God.

Arrows

The next picture of doctrine is *"the shooting of an arrow."* The interesting thing about this picture is that it seems always to be in the negative; for example, people who shoot a teaching to wound or harm. Look at the following as further examples.

> *Proverbs 26:18-19 Like a madman who **throws** Firebrands, arrows and death, So is the man who deceives his neighbor, And says, "Was I not joking?"*

*Psalm 64:3-7 Who have sharpened their tongue like a sword. They aimed bitter speech as their arrow, To **shoot** from concealment at the blameless; Suddenly they **shoot** at him, and do not fear. They hold fast to themselves an evil purpose; They talk of laying snares secretly; They say, "Who can see them?" They devise injustices, saying, "We are ready with a well-conceived plot"; For the inward thought and the heart of a man are deep. But God will **shoot** at them with an arrow; Suddenly they will be wounded.*

The reason this is important is that it brings clarity to another Scripture dealing with the spiritual warfare we are engaged in. When we understand true spiritual warfare, we begin to fight battles that are real, and we begin to see victories in the lives of those bound by the enemy to do his will.

*Ephesians 6:16 in addition to all, taking up the shield of faith with which you will be able to extinguish all the **flaming arrows** of the evil one.*

If the arrows are negative teachings or deceptions then we can see why the shield of faith will extinguish every one of them. God has given us the truth. Thus, when we come into agreement with the truth and then we hear a lie, the lie has no effect for the truth takes it captive. Your faith believes in what God has said to the point of action or fruit. It is the parable of the sower again.

Water

The third picture of doctrine is that of *"cleansing, washing, and watering."* What a beautiful word this is for it gives us three stark pictures of the importance of doctrine.

> **Proverbs 18:4** *The words of a man's mouth are deep waters; The fountain of wisdom is a bubbling brook.*

> **Hosea 6:3** *"So let us know, let us press on to know the Lord. His going forth is as certain as the dawn; And He will come to us like the rain, Like the spring rain **watering** the earth."*

> **Ephesians 5:25-27** *Husbands, love your wives, just as Christ also loved the church and gave Himself up for her, so that He might sanctify her, **having cleansed her by the washing of water with the word,** that He might present to Himself the church in all her glory, having no spot or wrinkle or any such thing; but that she would be holy and blameless.*

Doctrine resulted in our salvation. How is it that some can say that doctrine is not important? It is vital for salvation. The word *"teacher"* in the Hebrew means *"rain."* The teaching of the doctrines of God has the power to bring cleansing to the hearer if they will accept His words.

> **Isaiah 55:10-11** *"For as the rain and the snow come down from heaven, And do not return there without watering the earth And making it bear and sprout, And furnishing seed to the sower and bread*

to the eater; So will My word be which goes forth
from My mouth; It will not return to Me empty,
Without accomplishing what I desire, And without
succeeding in the matter for which I sent it.

God's words have a purpose behind them. They have a result in mind. It is found in the intention of God who spoke them. The effect is likened to that of rain and snow upon the earth. This is important because of the effect that water has upon a seed. There is an interesting law in the Bible concerning seed. If the dead carcass of an animal comes in contact with seed, that seed is NOT unclean. On the other hand, if the seed has been watered and the dead carcass comes in contact with it, the seed IS unclean.

This shows us that the seed is dead without the water. However, the moment you put water upon that seed, life comes into it and it begins to grow. When God sends His doctrine to us, it has the potential to bring alive that which was dead.

> *Isaiah 30:20-21 Although the Lord has given you*
> *bread of privation and water of oppression, He,*
> *your Teacher will no longer hide Himself, but your*
> *eyes will behold your Teacher. Your ears will hear*
> *a word behind you, "This is the way, walk in it,"*
> *whenever you turn to the right or to the left.*

Doctrine requires a teacher to teach it. Isaiah presents God as our Teacher. If He is our Teacher then what He teaches is important. The Bible is full of the teachings of God, how is it then that any of us can say that doctrine is not important or that we have had enough doctrine?

> *I Timothy 6:3-5 If anyone advocates a different*
> *doctrine and does not agree with sound words,*

*those of our Lord Jesus Christ, and with the doctrine conforming to godliness, **he is conceited and understands nothing**; but he has a morbid interest in controversial questions and disputes about words, out of which arise envy, strife, abusive language, evil suspicions, and constant friction between men of depraved mind and deprived of the truth, who suppose that godliness is a means of gain.*

Paul reveals to us that those that do not want to adhere to doctrine or sound words are actually conceited and they understand nothing. Every time I have heard a person say doctrine is not important, their life was usually marked by a lack of understanding and study. It was more of a justification of their own lack and they felt so inadequate that they needed to resort to bringing glory to themselves.

> **Romans 16:17** *Now I urge you, brethren, keep your eye on those who cause dissensions and hindrances contrary to the teaching which you learned, and turn away from them.*

It is amazing some of the things that are offered as sound doctrine. Not only must we be careful not to lapse into the idea that doctrine is not important, we must also be able to discern true doctrine from every wind of doctrine. That means we will have to study to show ourselves approved of God by rightly dividing the Word of God.

> **Matthew 15:9** *'But in vain do they worship Me, Teaching as doctrines the precepts of men.'* "

If teaching the precepts of men were vain worship, then that would mean that valid teaching is equal to true worship of God. Those that tell us that doctrine is no longer important are actually telling us that worship is no longer important!

> *I Timothy 4:13 Until I come, give attention to the public reading of Scripture, to exhortation and teaching.*

The way that verse reads in the Greek is as follows: *"Until I come hold to the reading, the encouragement, the teaching."* The verses that I am casting out there are showing us that doctrine is not only important, it is vital. The picture Paul paints is one that shows us that we need to *"HOLD"* on to solid teaching and doctrine, not cast it away. The problem of division is not doctrine—it is pride.

> *I Timothy 4:16 Pay close attention to yourself and to your teaching; persevere in these things, for as you do this you will ensure salvation both for yourself and for those who hear you.*

The Greek reads as follows: *"Hold on to yourself and to the teaching; stay on to them; this for doing both yourself you will deliver and the ones hearing you."*

> *II Timothy 3:16-17 All Scripture is inspired by God and profitable for teaching, for reproof, for correction, for training in righteousness; so that the man of God may be adequate, equipped for every good work.*

Need I say more?

Titus 1:9-11 holding fast the faithful word which is in accordance with the teaching, so that he will be able both to exhort in sound doctrine and to refute those who contradict. For there are many rebellious men, empty talkers and deceivers, especially those of the circumcision, who must be silenced because they are upsetting whole families, teaching things they should not teach for the sake of sordid gain.

Even more so today, are we faced with rebellious men who refuse to submit to discipleship and believe they could just teach themselves. In doing so, they have become empty talkers and deceivers.

Titus 2:7-8 in all things show yourself to be an example of good deeds, with purity in doctrine, dignified, sound in speech which is beyond reproach, so that the opponent will be put to shame, having nothing bad to say about us.

The point is made. Doctrine is indeed important and vital to a healthy Christian experience. Those that are lone rangers and refuse to study doctrine have opened themselves up to hear another gospel. They have placed themselves in the unattractive position of being deceived. Either we submit our self unto God and His ways, or we wander aimlessly through life thinking we are filled with truth, but actually, we become the proponent of lies.

I Timothy 4:1-2 But the Spirit explicitly says that in later times some will fall away from the faith, paying attention to deceitful spirits and doctrines of demons, by means of the hypocrisy of liars seared in their own conscience as with a branding iron,

It is interesting that people would say doctrine is not important and yet the devil sees his own doctrine as vital! We are in a time where even those in the Church are saying that we do not need any more doctrine. This is such a danger and I would even go on to say that it is in itself a doctrine of demons. The last thing the devil wants you to do is to read and study the Scriptures.

> **II Timothy 4:3-4** *For the time will come when they will not endure sound doctrine; but wanting to have their ears tickled, they will accumulate for themselves teachers in accordance to their own desires, and will turn away their ears from the truth and will turn aside to myths.*

The Greek reads as follows: *"...and from indeed the truth the hearing they will turn off; on but the myths they will be turned out."* There will be those who will literally turn off their hearing and they will be unable to hear the truth. However, to myths, they will open their ears and receive it. This is a condition of deception. They are already deceived and unable to hear the truth. Jesus experienced this as well.

> **John 8:43-44** *"Why do you not understand what I am saying?* **It is because you cannot hear My word.** *"You are of your father the devil, and you want to do the desires of your father. He was a murderer from the beginning, and does not stand in the truth because there is no truth in him. Whenever he speaks a lie, he speaks from his own nature, for he is a liar and the father of lies."*

"It is because you cannot hear My word..." Wow! Jesus revealed that when people are unable to hear the simple plain truth, they are of their father the devil who is a liar! Jesus was not talking

to simple folk here. He was talking to the leaders who had the knowledge of God at their fingertips.

If teaching and doctrine are so important what does that say about discipleship? If discipleship is the means by which we are filled with the knowledge of God, and that the knowledge of God is vital in our being stewards of the Word of God, then do you think that we should become disciples? Jesus modeled for us what He wanted us to continue after He had gone.

> *Matthew 28:19-20* *"Go therefore and make disciples of all the nations, baptizing them in the name of the Father and the Son and the Holy Spirit, teaching them to observe all that I commanded you; and lo, I am with you always, even to the end of the age."*

Jesus made disciples; He did not just make converts. He then told His disciples to do the same thing He had done. Go make disciples. Yet, most systems of evangelism today are centered on making converts. These converts are saved, but they do not understand the necessity to become a disciple of Jesus. They are then easy prey for the enemy to come steal the Word out of their hearts.

Jesus was modeling for all of us the system that He created, designed, and commanded to be followed; not only this, but there was already a system in place in the Hebrew culture where discipleship was a natural progression in growing up. Jesus does not ask us to do anything that He did not already model for us.

> *John 8:28-29* *So Jesus said, "When you lift up the Son of Man, then you will know that I am He, and I do nothing on My own initiative, but I speak these*

things as the Father taught Me. "And He who sent Me is with Me; He has not left Me alone, for I always do the things that are pleasing to Him."

This reveals to us that Jesus was taught. Most of us have thought that since Jesus was also God, He came preloaded with all of the knowledge of the universe. We forget that the Bible also says that Jesus emptied Himself and took on human flesh. Jesus was a blank slate and needed to be a disciple in order to become the Messiah. This may seem farfetched to you, but what other explanation is there for Jesus being taught?

The conclusion of this is that Jesus modeled not only being the Mentor or Teacher, but He also modeled being the Disciple. It was being a Disciple that qualified Him to become a Teacher. This next piece of Scripture has been heralded as a Messianic passage for centuries.

> *Isaiah 50:6-7 I gave My back to those who strike Me, And My cheeks to those who pluck out the beard; I did not cover My face from humiliation and spitting. For the Lord God helps Me, Therefore, I am not disgraced; Therefore, I have set My face like flint, And I know that I will not be ashamed.*

What you may not be familiar with is the two verses before that.

> *Isaiah 50:4-5 The Lord God has given Me the tongue of disciples, That I may know how to sustain the weary one with a word. He awakens Me morning by morning, He awakens My ear to listen as a disciple. The Lord God has opened My ear; And I was not disobedient Nor did I turn back.*

There it is; the Father was teaching Jesus as a Disciple. Nevertheless, I want you also to note the reason or outcome of being a disciple. The purpose of learning and of teaching is so you will be prepared to sustain the weary one with a word. This is why He was confounding the top scholars of His time at the age of twelve.

This presents us with the notion that true discipleship is a prerequisite for ministry. How many have actually become ministers without first being discipled? The next thing that must be understood is what it means to be a disciple. What do disciples do and what regimen would be equal to discipleship and what regimen would not be equal to discipleship? If we are going to understand this, we need to comprehend it through the culture of the Hebrews at the time Jesus was on the earth.

The Hebraic understanding of discipleship is much like that of an apprentice program. The disciple would choose a mentor and then spend untold hours learning from his mentor. It usually became a lifelong relationship as the mentor taught all that he had learned.

When Jesus discipled His twelve, He was imparting into them the things He learned from the Father. This is why Jesus said, *"I only say what I hear my Father saying."* This was the statement of the Disciple Jesus repeating what He had learned from His Father. In doing this, He was also teaching the twelve to be good disciples.

Look what He told His disciples. He commissioned them to go into all the world and make disciples teaching them to observe all that He commanded. In other words, Jesus was telling them to do the same thing He had done in their lives.

When we have a six-week course and call that discipleship, we cheapen greatly the true meaning of being a disciple. When the Apostle Paul said to study to show yourself approved of God, his meaning of study and our meaning of study need to be the same. We need to take into account the Hebraic culture to arrive at a truthful understanding of the Word.

The Hebrew word for study is to rub, to beat, to tread, to trample. It gives us the picture that there is much effort engaged in extracting the revelation from the text. How lazy we have become with videos, CDs, tapes and such. We turn on the TV and get a sermon to feel like we have applied ourselves. There is much more to it than that.

Replicating The Anointing

I n the Hebrew mindset the whole purpose of being a disciple is to become like your mentor. In Christianity we are to become like Jesus; He is actually our Mentor. We are disciples of Messiah. That does not eliminate humans from being mentors; it only means that all mentors should be teaching their disciples to be imitators of Christ. Paul made the statement to his disciples to follow him as he followed Christ. They were to be built into the image of Christ, not the image of Paul.

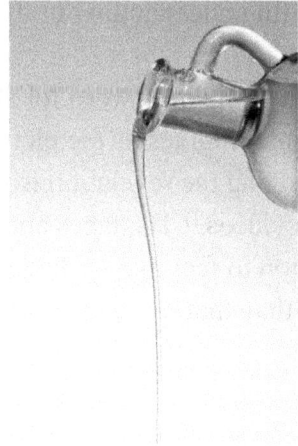

When disciples began separating along the lines of their teachers, i.e. *"I am of Apollos, I am of Paul, I am of Christ,"* Paul rebuked them. We are the Body of Messiah not another person or denomination. We are being transformed into His image not the image of another. We are no longer to build ministries after ourselves, but after Christ alone. It is therefore necessary for all Christian mentors to point their disciples to Jesus.

The language used in the New Testament must be coupled with an understanding of the terms as they were used in that time. To be transformed into the image of another is actually the picture of being a disciple. In the Hebraic culture, there was the pursuit of the disciple to be exactly like the mentor. They would put great energy in becoming like their mentors.

Since we are disciples of Messiah, we are being changed or transformed into His image. That means that every mentor is to make it their charge to bring their disciples to the place where they are being transformed into the image of Jesus not the image of the mentor. The fact that the apostles understood this is found in the statement revealing our transformation into Christ.

Paul reveals in Ephesians chapter four, that Jesus' ministers were given to equip the saints for the work of God. Note that Paul used the term of attaining the measure of the stature that belongs to the fullness of Christ. Paul saw the whole purpose of discipleship as a means to bring the pupil to the measure of their Mentor Jesus. That means there had to be a transfer of anointing through that process. Messiah is Hebrew for the Anointed One, as Christ is the Greek for the Anointed One. If we are to attain the measure of the stature that belongs to Christ, then we must be anointed in and through the process of discipleship.

How many people have forgone discipleship and as a result have forgone anointing? Without the anointing, we are incapable of setting the captive free, of proclaiming good news to the poor, or of proclaiming the favorable year of the Lord. Jesus said that He was anointed to do those things; do we actually think that we could do those things without the anointing? Moreover, do we actually think that we can get the anointing to do such things without undergoing the process of being discipled?

> **Genesis 1:11-12** *Then God said, "Let the earth sprout vegetation, plants yielding seed, and fruit trees on the earth bearing fruit after their kind with seed in them"; and it was so. The earth brought forth vegetation, plants yielding seed after their kind, and trees bearing fruit with seed in them, after their kind; and God saw that it was good.*

Physical replication has always been done through the seed principle. It is a physical law I believe, that is transfused into the spiritual as well. Jesus likens:

- Faith to a mustard seed
- The Word of God to sowing seed
- The spiritual consequences of sin and righteousness to sowing and reaping
- Giving to sowing and reaping

It seems that when we talk about replication there has to be a seed involved and there must be something sowed. When God created man and woman, He said,

> **Genesis 1:27-28** *God created man in His own image, in the image of God He created him; male and female He created them. God blessed them; and God said to them, "Be fruitful and multiply, and fill the earth, and subdue it; and rule over the fish of the sea and over the birds of the sky and over every living thing that moves on the earth."*

When it comes to the anointing, I believe that we have the ability to replicate it or pass it on, but with some conditions that must be met first. Our God is a generous God, but He is also a benevolent God. He will not be generous with His anointing if it will harm us. We must be prepared to receive it so that we will not take glory unto ourselves.

It seems to be the pattern of God that He starts something and gives it the power to continue and to grow. This is the picture of the seed again. God did not plan to recreate a tree every time one died. He put within the tree the power of multiplication to keep it going. When He created man, God did not create more than the man and the woman for in them was the power to multiply and fill the earth.

Likewise, I believe the anointing has a beginning and it has the power to be passed on from generation to generation. That families and individuals are called to fulfill a purpose and thereby build a name for God in the earth. I think that we can see a picture of this in the anointing of the Levitical priesthood.

> **Exodus 29:7** *"Then you shall take the anointing oil and pour it on his head and anoint him.*

> **Leviticus 8:30** *So Moses took some of the anointing oil and some of the blood which was on the altar and sprinkled it on Aaron, on his garments, on his sons, and on the garments of his sons with him; and he consecrated Aaron, his garments, and his sons, and the garments of his sons with him.*

It should be noted that the anointing oil was a special mixture of olive oil and spices that was to be one of a kind. God gave instructions not to make it for any other purpose then for God's stated purpose. It is also interesting that God said in Exodus 30:33, that if anyone anoints a layman or stranger that they shall be cut off from the people. This shows us that the anointing is not just for anyone, but those that have gone through the correct procedure or process, which is discipleship.

> **Psalm 133** *Behold, how good and how pleasant it is For brothers to dwell together in unity! It is like the precious oil upon the head, Coming down upon the beard, Even Aaron's beard, Coming down upon the*

*edge of his robes. It is like the dew of Hermon
Coming down upon the mountains of Zion; For
there the Lord commanded the blessing—life
forever.*

This is the beginning of the Levitical and Aaronic priesthood. Note that it begins with the anointing by a prophet (Moses) and with the oil. The prophetic ministry is tasked with awakening the call of God upon a life. The blessing that is proclaimed through the anointing is life forever.

What a dynamic picture of ministry that God would command the blessing of life forever. Not only that, but it is a declaration of Christ and His sacrifice that is the only means of life forever. Remember, Christ means anointed. Priests were not the only ones anointed in the Bible. Kings were also anointed.

*I Samuel 16:13 Then Samuel took the horn of oil
and anointed him in the midst of his brothers; and
the Spirit of the Lord came mightily upon David
from that day forward. And Samuel arose and went
to Ramah.*

There is a significant difference though. Samuel poured oil upon Saul, the first King of Israel, and the Spirit of God came upon Saul. However, when God rejected Saul as King and chose David instead, it required another anointing. Right after David is anointed with oil, the Spirit of God came upon David and in verse fourteen, we find that the Spirit of God left Saul. It was not this way with the priesthood. There was only one anointing with oil and that was upon Aaron. The anointing was passed down through the line of Levi from generation to generation.

Why would new kings require a new anointing, but new priests could have it transferred to them? I suppose it could be argued that because of the failure of Saul that the kingly call passed to another tribe and thus required a new anointing. However, even in the line of David, all new kings underwent anointing with oil. I think that we can find the answer in the notion that God had never ordained that man should have a king.

This was diametrically opposed to the plan of God. This notion was not the government that God had chosen for His people. God was supposed to have been their King. Because of this rejection of God's structure, His grace was needed EVERY time a king took office. As a result, the anointing was not passed down from king to king as it was from priest to priest.

> **Numbers 20:25-29** *"Take Aaron and his son Eleazar and bring them up to Mount Hor; and strip Aaron of his garments and put them on his son Eleazar. So Aaron will be gathered to his people, and will die there." So Moses did just as the Lord had commanded, and they went up to Mount Hor in the sight of all the congregation. After Moses had stripped Aaron of his garments and put them on his son Eleazar, Aaron died there on the mountain top. Then Moses and Eleazar came down from the mountain. When all the congregation saw that Aaron had died, all the house of Israel wept for Aaron thirty days.*

Contrast the anointing of the kings with the anointing of the priests. God sanctioned one (the priesthood) and man sanctioned the other (the king). The one sanctioned by man needed to have a fresh anointing when they took office. The one sanctioned by God was passed on from generation to generation through the mantle.

In God's system, there was a necessity of fathers passing on their mantle and anointing to the sons. In man's system, there was no mantle to pass on. Each time a king took the position of king, they needed their head and their garment anointed again. This shows that when we follow God's system of things, there will be the natural transference of anointing and mantles from the fathers to the sons. It was the garment of Aaron that had the oil stains upon it that was passed down to the sons of Aaron.

We have two lines of anointing. There is the anointing of the priesthood and there is the anointing of the king. Notice that both need sons to keep both these lines of anointing alive. There is a spiritual principle to be learned here. The anointing is kept alive by the sons. I believe this counts both physically and spiritually. It is called *"the birthright."* From the spiritual aspect, we see a great picture of the need for sons to keep the anointing alive in the father and son relationship between Elijah and Elisha.

> *Malachi 4:5-6 "Behold, I am going to send you Elijah the prophet before the coming of the great and terrible day of the Lord. He will restore the hearts of the fathers to their children and the hearts of the children to their fathers, so that I will not come and smite the land with a curse."*

T.L. Lowery said, *"The purpose of sending Elijah the prophet in the last days is because Elijah was the only person in the Old Testament who successfully reproduced himself in ministry."* Reproduction means that there is a full transference of mantle and anointing from the spiritual father to the spiritual son. It should also be noted that without son-ship or father-ship there is no transference of mantle or anointing. What does this say of people who have gone into ministry and have not submitted to the process of discipleship?

Those verses in Malachi are the last two verses in the Old Testament. God ends the first covenant with a promise of hope for the second. The New Testament opens with the coming of John the Baptist. John is a partial fulfillment of that Scripture in Malachi for Jesus says of John:

> *Matthew 11:14 And if you are willing to receive it, he (John) is Elijah who is to come. (emphasis is mine)*

The necessity of us to understand the import of being spiritual sons and fathers cannot be underscored. Elijah has the anointing to turn the hearts of fathers to the sons and the sons to the fathers precisely because he himself modeled father-ship.

> *Luke 1:15-17 "For he will be great in the sight of the Lord; and he will drink no wine or liquor, and he will be filled with the Holy Spirit while yet in his mother's womb. "And he will turn many of the sons of Israel back to the Lord their God. "It is he who will go as a forerunner before Him in the spirit and power of Elijah, to turn the hearts of the fathers back to the children, and the disobedient to the attitude of the righteous, so as to make ready a people prepared (equipped) for the Lord."*

This description of Elijah's ministry is very close to Ephesians 4:11-12, which describes the ministry of the five fold. When held in this light we are led to the idea that Elijah was a forerunner of the ministry Jesus would institute at His ascension. If this is true, then the five ministries of apostle, prophet, teacher, pastor, and evangelist are tasked to make disciples for the purpose of preparing them for the Lord and their ministries. Elisha, the disciple of Elijah, was not forbidden from being in the vicinity of the Lord's taking of Elijah and he received the mantle and anointing in a double portion.

> ***Psalm 127:1-5*** *Unless the Lord builds the house, They labor in vain who build it; Unless the Lord guards the city, The watchman stays awake in vain. It is vain for you to rise up early, To sit up late, To eat the bread of sorrows; For so He gives His beloved sleep.* ***Behold, children are a heritage from the Lord****, The fruit of the womb is a reward. Like arrows in the hand of a warrior, So are the children of one's youth. Happy is the man who has his quiver full of them; They shall not be ashamed, But shall speak with their enemies in the gate.*

Sons are an inheritance from the Lord. There is assumed purpose in that statement! That is that God gives children to carry on the call or mantle upon a family or ministry. Even Jesus mentioned that the Father gave His disciples to Him. Disciples are sons and daughters that are to be mantled and anointed by their spiritual fathers so that they can take the father's anointing into the future. Note also that the building of a house or ministry by God requires fathers and sons. The establishment of a ministry is done through the sons and daughters given to that ministry.

> ***Exodus 29:29-30*** *"And the* ***holy garments*** *(mantle) of Aaron shall be his sons' after him, to be anointed in them and to be consecrated in them. That son who becomes priest in* ***his place*** *shall put them on for seven days, when he enters the tabernacle of*

meeting to minister in the holy place. (emphasis is mine)

This is the physical transference of anointing. The number seven is significant in that it stands for perfection or completion. We could also say *"maturity."* The purpose of the five fold ministry is to mature the saints. Walking in the anointed mantle for seven days was a picture of the transfer of anointing upon a completed or matured disciple. We also have a picture of spiritual transference of anointing in the story of Elijah and Elisha.

> *I Kings 19:15-16 Then the Lord said to him: "Go, return on your way to the Wilderness of Damascus; and when you arrive, anoint Hazael as king over Syria. Also you shall anoint Jehu the son of Nimshi as king over Israel. And Elisha the son of Shaphat of Abel Meholah you shall anoint as prophet in your place.*

These were three distinct commands given to Elijah by God. What should be noted though is that Elijah only completed the last one mentioned. Elisha, Elijah's spiritual son, completed the other two mentioned. How many ministries have died with their founders because there were no sons to carry on the mantle and anointing of that ministry? Look at how Elijah anointed Elisha.

> *I Kings 19:19 So he departed from there, and found Elisha the son of Shaphat, who was plowing with twelve yoke of oxen before him, and he was with the twelfth. Then Elijah passed by him and threw his **mantle** on him.*

The anointing of Elisha began with the mantle of Elijah being put upon Elisha. This was the invitation to become a disciple in order to carry on the ministry of Elijah. Elisha could have refused. However, if he was to be who God created and purposed him to be, he would need to be a disciple in order to capture that mantle and anointing. When the sons of Aaron walked in his mantle, they in a sense captured the call of Aaron. They were also showing that they were submitting to a higher call. They no longer were committed to their own ministries or their own desires, but they were taking upon themselves the very purpose for which they were created and by doing so, they positioned themselves to be used of God in a powerful and dynamic way.

Elisha was not completely anointed when Elijah threw his mantle upon him. It was only the beginning of his ministry. It was an invitation to carry the burden or call that Elijah had received of the Lord. Oh my God in heaven, give us sons and fathers for the glory of Your kingdom!

> *I Kings 19:21 So Elisha turned back from him, and took a yoke of oxen and slaughtered them and boiled their flesh, using the oxen's equipment, and gave it to the people, and they ate. Then he arose and followed Elijah, and became his servant.*

Observe that Elisha completely forsook his current state and occupation and threw himself into the purpose of God. If we are to become what God has ordained, it is going to require an initiative on our part to forsake some things in our own lives.

When we follow these two people, we find that Elisha serves Elijah. This is a paradigm and pattern for receiving the anointing. Elisha was to work and serve his mentor in order to capture the vision and anointing of his mentor. If we are not willing to be servants to those who have watch over our souls, we are not ready for leadership. What was the reputation of the disciple Elisha?

> **II Kings 3:11** *But Jehoshaphat said, "Is there no prophet of the Lord here, that we may inquire of the Lord by him?" So one of the servants of the king of Israel answered and said,* **"Elisha the son of Shaphat is here, who poured water on the hands of Elijah."**

Elisha had the reputation for service unto Elijah his mentor. As far as that servant was concerned, Elisha was just a servant. Jesus did not come to be served but to serve. Who are we that we should not do likewise? What was the culmination of this service? Rewind to when Elijah is being taken away by God.

> **II Kings 2:9** *And so it was, when they had crossed over, that Elijah said to Elisha, "Ask! What may I do for you, before I am taken away from you?" Elisha said, "Please let a double portion of your spirit be upon me."*

This term *"double portion"* is a family term between a father and son. The first-born son was to get a double portion of inheritance from the father. Here we find again that there is an inheritance aspect between the father and the son spiritually.

> **Deuteronomy 21:17** *But he shall acknowledge the son of the unloved wife as the firstborn by giving him a double portion of all that he has, for he is the* **beginning of his strength**; *the right of the firstborn is his.*

The purpose of the double portion was that it signified the beginning of the strength of that father. This means that the call, anointing, mantle, and work of that father was to be continued and expanded in the life of the son. There was to be a growth aspect to this transference.

The Hebrew word for *"portion"* means mouth and the Hebrew root word for mouth means, *"to blow."* This will become significantly important as we proceed. Elijah told Elisha that he asks a hard thing, but then Elijah gives the conditions upon which this transference of anointing will take place.

> ***II Kings 2:10*** *So he said, "You have asked a hard thing. Nevertheless, if you **see** me when I am taken from you, it shall be so for you; but if not, it shall not be so."*

This was not a condition of receiving the anointing but it was simply a sign that he had received it. Seeing Elijah being taken up was just proof. This is significant because it speaks of the faithfulness of the disciple that they would follow their mentor until they leave this earth. Father and son relationships do not change when the son grows up and then moves away to start his own life. When the son comes back to visit the father, the terms of the relationship have not changed. A father is a father for life and a son is a son for life. Notice also Elisha's response to Elijah's departure.

> ***II Kings 2:11-13*** *Then it happened, as they continued on and talked, that suddenly a chariot of fire appeared with horses of fire, and separated the two of them; and Elijah went up by a whirlwind into heaven. And Elisha saw it, and he cried out, "**My father, my father**, the chariot of Israel and its horsemen!" So he saw him no more. And he took hold of his own clothes and tore them into two pieces. He also took up the mantle of Elijah that*

had fallen from him, and went back and stood by
the bank of the Jordan.

Look at Elisha's response. He cried out, *"My father, my*
father!" Elisha understood the mentor relationship that he had with
Elijah. Elisha saw Elijah as his spiritual father. Are we at a place in
Christianity where we no longer need fathers in the faith? We still
need to be discipled and we still need to be fathered. The process
of being discipled may be lacking in your life. If it is, I encourage
you to enter into discipleship.

The tearing of Elisha's own clothes and the taking up of
Elijah's mantle was a picture of the son taking up the burden and
vision of the spiritual father to the removal of his own will and
desires to carry on the ministry of his spiritual father. Did Elisha
get that double portion? Well, he saw his mentor being taken up.
Observe also that Elisha had twice as many miracles recorded in
the Bible as Elijah had.

The reason that I wanted to spend so much time on this subject
is that it is a pattern that is repeated in the New Testament. When
Jesus chose twelve disciples it was not something new taking
place. The Hebrew culture was replete with the idea of being
discipled. What many people are not aware of is that Jesus was
also a Disciple before He became a Mentor. His Father taught
Him. When Jesus reached the age of ministry (thirty), John
baptized Him in the Jordan. Look at what happens at this important
event.

> ***John 8:28*** *So Jesus said, "When you lift up the Son*
> *of Man, then you will know that I am He, and I do*
> *nothing on My own initiative, but I speak these*
> *things as the Father taught Me.*

Many people think that Jesus came preloaded with all knowledge and understanding because He was God in the flesh. However, it is said of Jesus that He emptied Himself and took on the form of a servant. It was necessary to teach Jesus, and His Father God did just that. This idea is also found in Isaiah.

> **Isaiah 50:6** *I gave My back to those who strike Me, And My cheeks to those who pluck out the beard; I did not cover My face from humiliation and spitting.*

I quote this verse to substantiate that this portion of Scripture is Messianic. Now if we back up two verses, note what is said.

> **Isaiah 50:4-5** *The Lord God has given Me the tongue of disciples, That I may know how to sustain the weary one with a word. He awakens Me morning by morning, He awakens My ear to listen as a disciple. The Lord God has opened My ear; And I was not disobedient Nor did I turn back.*

Before Jesus was a Mentor, He was a disciple. This means if He was a successful Disciple that He carries the vision, mantle, and anointing of His Father at the time He is commissioned by the Father and sent out as a Mentor.

> **Matthew 3:16** *After being baptized, Jesus came up immediately from the water; and behold, the heavens were opened, and he saw the Spirit of God descending as a dove and lighting on Him,*

The Spirit of God came upon Him. This is important because the Bible declares that fullness of the Godhead dwelled in Him in bodily form. This means that the Spirit was **in Him**, but it **did not**

come upon Him until His baptism. If we watch what happens after this we can find that the Spirit of God anointed Him.

> *Luke 4:14-20 And Jesus returned to Galilee in the power of the Spirit, and news about Him spread through all the surrounding district. And He began teaching in their synagogues and was praised by all. And He came to Nazareth, where He had been brought up; and as was His custom, He entered the synagogue on the Sabbath, and stood up to read. And the book of the prophet Isaiah was handed to Him. And He opened the book and found the place where it was written, "The Spirit of the Lord is upon Me, Because **He anointed Me** to preach the gospel to the poor. He has sent Me to proclaim release to the captives, And recovery of sight to the blind, To set free those who are oppressed, To proclaim the favorable year of the Lord." And He closed the book, gave it back to the attendant and sat down; and the eyes of all in the synagogue were fixed on Him.*

The Spirit was UPON Him BECAUSE He ANOINTED Me to… The sons of Aaron would walk with the mantle of Aaron upon them for seven days in a transference of anointing. How would God Who is Spirit transfer His anointing to His Disciple Jesus? It would be by Spirit. The Spirit of God became the mantle of God that is inherited by the Son. Jesus was a disciple and the moment it was time for Him to enter into His ministry, the Spirit from the Father anoints him! Now at the end of Jesus' ministry we find that Jesus repeated this pattern.

> *John 20:21-22 So Jesus said to them again, "Peace be with you; as the Father has sent Me, **I also send***

you." *And when He had said this,* **He breathed** *on them and said to them, "Receive the Holy Spirit."*

Remember that the root Hebrew word for *"portion"* means, *"to blow?"* The physical mantle has become a spiritual one. This took place after the resurrection of Jesus. He faithfully passed on the anointing to His disciples as the Father passed on the anointing to His Son. Jesus replicated the anointing.

The picture is clear, that if one will become a disciple, they position themselves to receive an anointing to take up their spiritual father's ministry. Jesus told His disciples to go make disciples. He wanted them to repeat the process! Note what Jesus said to His disciples. He said the works that I do, you shall do, and greater works than these shall you do. In addition, the disciples watched Jesus ascend just as Elisha watched Elijah ascend. Because of this, I believe that they carried a double portion of anointing.

What happens when a spiritual father refuses to be a father, or a spiritual son refuses to be a son? The anointing stops and is not passed on. This is a sad condition. How many have forfeited, even ignorantly, the process, and as a result they are unable to carry the anointing and mantle that God had designed for them?

Elisha had a double portion of Elijah's anointing. Who then could have received that anointing from Elisha? Before we answer that we must ask the question, *"Is there a sign that shows that Elisha did not pass on the anointing but carried that anointing to the grave?"*

II Kings 13:20-21 *Then Elisha died, and they buried him. And the raiding bands from Moab invaded the land in the spring of the year. So it was,*

as they were burying a man, that suddenly they
spied a band of raiders; and they put the man in the
tomb of Elisha; and when the man was let down and
touched the bones of Elisha, he revived and stood
on his feet.

Could it be that this was a proof that the anointing of Elijah was still in his bones? We do not know why Elisha did not pass on and replicate the anointing; nevertheless, there were no disciples of his who took the mantle of Elijah in order to continue Elisha's ministry. Elisha's servant was Eleazar and he apparently did not carry the passion for carrying that mantle as Elisha did. In fact, Eleazar was struck with leprosy because of the issue with Naman. We do not know for sure why this was not accomplished. However, the Apostle Paul alludes to the problem of passing on the anointing.

Philippians 2:20-22 *For I have no one **like-minded**, who will sincerely care for your state. For all seek their own, not the things which are of Christ Jesus. But you know his proven character, that as a son with his father he served with me in the gospel.*

Paul was talking about his disciple, Timothy. Notice the same elements of a good disciple are that he served him as a son would a father. The bottom line is this: Without discipleship and fathering, the anointing is not replicated. If we spurn discipleship, we are not doing justice to the call of God upon the lives of those who were to carry an anointing to do mighty miracles.

If you are not a disciple, then you need to find the spiritual father that God has connected you with, or allow them to find you. Do not resist when you find them, but assist them and give yourself to pour water upon their hands in service. If you do not, you cannot expect the anointing to be replicated in your life. I believe this is why we have a shortage of miracles in the Church today. There has not been replication of anointing taking place. We must correct this, follow God's wise plan, and start replicating the anointing if we are to see the works of Jesus again in the Church.

In the next chapter, we are going to look at what it means to capture your identity so that you can enter into what God has for you. Once you do enter in, you can protect what God has given to you. As you enter into the process of discipleship you are not becoming a disciple of a man or woman, you are becoming a disciple of Jesus. There are two reasons why it is important to grasp that idea.

First, man can only pass the anointing on physically as in the case of family anointings. We need to be a disciple of Jesus in order to be anointed with His anointing which is His Spirit. That does not suggest that once the Spirit comes upon us we are automatically discipled. If that were the case, then there would have been no need for the five fold ministry.

Second, remember that Elijah threw his mantle upon Elisha at the beginning of his discipleship. Likewise, God throws His mantle upon us at the beginning of our discipleship. Then at the time of maturity, there is another anointing by the laying on of hands by the presbytery as they did to Paul and Barnabas in the book of Acts as they were being sent out.

DESTINY SERIES 201

Identity vs. Individualism

D iscipleship is really defined in finding one's true identity. The problem is that many mistake individualism for identity. I was in a restaurant one evening and as I am oft to do, I look at the things that they put on the walls. In this one particular restaurant, there was a quote by George Bernard Shaw.

> *Life isn't about finding yourself. Life is about creating yourself.*
> *--George Bernard Shaw*

I thought to myself, *"What a statement that defines the time we live in today."* The question that arises in my mind is, *"Is that statement a true statement?"* **If it is true, then we need only to create the image that we want to portray to generate the response or end result that we want.** I am afraid that too many ministers have already traveled that road. If we are creating our image for the purpose of generating an end result, then no matter how noble the end result, the means to that end amounts to manipulation and witchcraft.

If we are to understand our self, we need to find our true identity. It is one of the fundamental questions of life. *"Who am I?"* As children we have our identity through our parents. In our ascendency to adulthood, that identity no longer satisfies us as human beings. We realize that there is more to us than what we were aware of as children. All of us have a mother and a father, but there is a spiritual quality to us that cannot be defined in physical terms nor explained in physical parents. We find identity as children through the similarities that we see in ourselves that are also in our parents. We have a sense of belonging because of this.

When we get to our teen years, we start desiring something more. We may not understand it, but we seek to find our true selves. Why? It is because men and women are not just physical beings but spiritual. As children, we are only aware of our physical nature. In growing up, we start down a road of dissatisfaction with regard to identity because of the intuitive knowledge that we are more than flesh. However, one cannot get their spirit from mere flesh or physical means. A spirit has no physical properties, it is without DNA, it is without form, it is invisible, yet it is more alive than physical things.

This means that we not only have physical parents, but we also must have a spiritual Parent. If my physical parents are only able to supply physical material for my physical being, then Who is my spiritual Father? The answer to that question will decide whether you capture the knowledge of your true self. This quest is a necessary one for all people.

The Word of God tells us that God is the Father of all spirits. The Bible also tells us that God is Spirit and they that worship Him must worship Him in spirit and truth. If God is Spirit then it makes sense that His children are spirits as well. I do not want this to lead to a belief that all are saved. The belief for example, that God created all human spirits therefore we are all children of God. Being a child of God by nature and being a child of God by choice are two different things.

Even though I have a physical father, I could have distanced myself from him and even considered him non-existent. I might be his child by nature, but I would not be his child by relationship. Likewise, it is with God. We must understand that He cannot deny us as His children, but we can deny Him as Father. He will not force us to be His children relationally.

It makes sense then, that if I do not find my true identity with God my Father, I am missing a necessary component in my existence and I will find a dissatisfaction that becomes hard to define and impossible to fix. It is because of this, as adults, identity with our parents is not enough to satisfy the need for identity.

Here is the problem though. When faced with this spiritual identity crisis, people often try to create themselves, thinking that they are finding their identity. Alternatively, they become attracted to the dark side of the spiritual world. An interesting Scripture states that Satan is the god of this age. It is interesting that the *"age"* is marked by different trends and styles. The enemy seeks to make it easy for human beings to think that if they can just make themselves different that they have achieved identity.

If you haven't noticed, each generation of young adults tries to define themselves in terms that separate them from the previous generation and their parents. We find that the advertisers have noticed this truth. If they can create the cultural difference that will be picked up by the current generation to define themselves apart from the previous generation, they can become billionaires. They are in full agreement with a generation identifying themselves. Although, in a truth they are only achieving individualism.

Individualism may look good and sound good, but it cannot ultimately satisfy the soul's need for identity. God created us to know Him. We have that spark of the divine that we call our spirit. We are not divine; we are not gods. God created us in His image to bear His likeness. Since the Bible tells us that God is Spirit and those that worship Him must worship Him in spirit and in truth, the only way that I am going to be able to identify with my spiritual Father, is to come to know Him by and through my spirit. The problem with coming to know my Creator is that I have been separated from Him by my own will and actions.

> *Ezekiel 18:4* *"Behold, all souls are Mine; the soul of the father as well as the soul of the son is Mine. The soul who sins will die.*

Since the Bible says of us all that we have sinned, we are all in a state of death. We are unable to know Him Who created us. We have an identity crisis. Because of this crisis, we seek for ways to satisfy our soul's need for identity and we wind up delving into things that only bring a momentary satisfaction. God provided a way for us to be reconciled with Him as our Parent. This was the goal and mission of Jesus. Look at the language Jesus uses.

> *John 3:1-3* *Now there was a man of the Pharisees, named Nicodemus, a ruler of the Jews; this man came to Jesus by night and said to Him, "Rabbi, we know that You have come from God as a teacher; for no one can do these signs that You do unless God is with him." Jesus answered and said to him, "Truly, truly, I say to you, unless one is born again* **he cannot see the kingdom of God.***"*

Jesus speaks of a new birth, a birth so dynamic that it allows me to find identity with my true spiritual Father. Could it be that all of the slanders that have been leveled at the term *"born again"* are actually dismissing the only way that we can find and access our identity? If so, how deceived has humankind become that they would see in a negative light their own road to identity.

> **John 3:4-7** *Nicodemus said to Him, "How can a man be born when he is old? He cannot enter a second time into his mother's womb and be born, can he?" Jesus answered, "Truly, truly, I say to you, unless one is born of water and the Spirit he cannot enter into the kingdom of God. "That which is born of the flesh is flesh, and that which is born of the Spirit is spirit. "Do not be amazed that I said to you, 'You must be born again.'*

Here we see the two possible identities. That which is born of the flesh is flesh. That is the identity that you have with your parents. They supplied the seed that resulted in the formation of your body. Your hair color, eye color, the shape of your nose and ears, and your height, are all physical traits that you inherited from your physical parents.

Then we have that which is born of the Spirit is spirit. God supplies the seed that resulted in you being a spiritual being. This means that you have inherited certain qualities from your spiritual Father in your Spirit.

The problem with this is that the soul that sins shall die. We have sinned and we are in need of a rebirth before we can be connected to our true identity. God provides this rebirth through our faith in His Son's death and resurrection. The moment we believed, we were born again and the seed of God came again into our spirits.

Oswald Chambers once said that individualism is all elbows. In other words, it pushes all others to the side in the attempt to stand out and be different. Individualism separates and isolates in the attempt to stand out from the crowd. We exist as an individual; however, we do not find identity in ourselves alone. The individual exists, but simply as the shell that holds the spirit, and it is the spirit that has a temperament. Temperament is the characteristic disposition of the spirit man, whereas individuality is the characteristic of the disposition of the natural man.

The temperament of each human comes with a disposition. Dispositions are the set ways of your temperament. That means that there are definitive traits with regard to your spirit that your Father created in you. Understanding this leads us to the knowledge that our disposition is fit perfectly for our destiny. We are made in such a way that we are to be excellent at fulfilling our destiny for which we were created. Each of us has traits of our spiritual Father. Our temperament then is the spiritual DNA of our spirit man.

When we lack true identity with our spiritual Father, the individual will try to counterfeit the temperament or true self. Because there is the intuitive knowledge in each of us that we are unique, we seek ways to be different from anyone else. If we try to be that which we truly are then we are no longer truly us. What I mean by that is we are who we are by nature of God's creation. We cannot change our temperaments with its disposition no more than you can change your height. Because you are unique, your identity must stand out as different then all others, but not through individualism.

What is the difference you might ask? When we substitute individualism for identity, we try to be different then what is common in our culture by creating an image of who we think we are or would like to be. We are trying to produce something so very different than what we see around us that we take drastic steps toward standing out. However, **identity can only be realized in emergence with another**. This is completely contrary to individualism. Individualism seeks to separate from all others. When you were identified with your family, your mergence with them is what created your identity.

John 10:30 *"I and the Father are one."*

Jesus modeled identity not individualism. He was completely merged with His Father. He had no psychological need to stand out from the crowd by creating His own image. Instead, He naturally stood out from the crowd by being merged with the Father that demonstrated an identity so unique that others noticed the difference. You too will stand out from the crowd as you begin to merge with your spiritual Father by being conformed into the image of His Son, Jesus.

John 5:30 *"I can do nothing on My own initiative. As I hear, I judge; and My judgment is just, because I do not seek My own will, but the will of Him who sent Me.*

The person who has true identity has no need to stand out from the crowd, yet because they are unique they will stand out. Life satisfaction then is reliant on us finding true identity. Without identity, we will always be unsatisfied since we will intuitively be aware that we do not know who we are, but not necessarily consciously. There will be that nagging question, *"Who am I?"* tugging at the soul.

Genesis 17:4-8 *"As for Me, behold, My covenant is with you, And you will be the father of a multitude of nations. "No longer shall your name be called Abram, But your name shall be Abraham; For I will*

make you the father of a multitude of nations. "I
have made you exceedingly fruitful, and I will make
nations of you, and kings will come forth from you.
"I will establish My covenant between Me and you
and your descendants after you throughout their
generations for an everlasting covenant, to be God
to you and to your descendants after you. "I will
give to you and to your descendants after you, the
land of your sojournings, all the land of Canaan,
for an everlasting possession; and I will be their
God. "

What is interesting about this passage is that it is a picture of the mergence of temperament with Another (God) and as a result, there was a name change (true identity). This shows that there was a shift from Abram the individual, to Abraham the friend of God.

We can see from the difference of the meaning of those two names. Abram means, *"exalted father."* Abram was an individualistic name that was individualistic in meaning, especially for someone who had no children. Abraham means *"father of a multitude."* In the name *"Abraham,"* we find mergence. Abraham is who he really is. When destiny met Abram, he became *"Abraham."* Abram was only a sense of greatness, but without definition. When a person has a sense of their purpose, but without definition, they will try to accomplish that vision in the flesh of their mind.

Another interesting bit of information is that the name change only resulted in the addition of a single Hebrew letter. Abram in Hebrew was composed of the Aleph, Beth, Resh, and Meem. Each Hebrew letter is also a picture. Abba is father in Hebrew.

The Aleph is a picture of the Ox Head; the Beth is the picture of House. Head of the house is the idea behind Abba. The *"Ab"* portion of Abram is Father. Therefore, the *"rm"* (there are no vowels in Hebrew) portion means exalted. The only letter added to change his name is the Ha (pronounced *"hay"*). The name *"exalted father"* points back into the past because that is the name given Abram at birth. It actually points back to Abram's father.

Interestingly, the letter Ha is the picture of a window. Add a window to the future and prophetically Abram becomes Abraham. The exalted father of the past becomes the father of a multitude in the future.

Sarah, Abraham's wife, also had a name change. Her name was Sarai (pronounced Saw-rah-ee) and it meant, *"nobility."* This time God removes the last letter of her name and again adds the *"Ha."* The letter that was taken away and replaced is the *"Yodh"* which is a picture of a *"hand."*

Here is the story that I think emerges. By removing the *"hand,"* God is showing that human effort cannot produce what you need to find identity. That would amount to individualism. By replacing it with the *"window,"* there is now a prophetic view into her true identity and she is freed to become who God created her to be. Sarah means, *"to place in order."* The picture is clear. When you allow your destiny to drive your purpose, and you surrender to it and enter into discipleship, you are placing your life in order.

Being born again is not some simple metaphor that has become the scourge of the world. You may not get a name change when you connect with your God through Jesus, but you will get a new nature. You will become who you were created to be by connecting to the only One who can define you and reveal your true purpose!

Galatians 4:29 But as at that time he who was born according to the flesh persecuted him who was born according to the Spirit, so it is now also.

When you operate out of individualism, you try to build your own destiny, but when you operate out of your spirit, you allow your destiny to unfold. Abram tried to force the promise of God by his own attempts. He had fathered a son through Sarah's handmaiden, Hagar, as Abram. Sarai actually initiated this, which shows her hand in the attempt to build by human effort. Abram was trying to build his identity by his own effort, but he only produced individualism.

It wasn't until his name was changed to Abraham by his spiritual Father, God, that he began to see his identity through His Father God and entered into faith regarding his future. It was only after the discovery of his true identity that he had the son of promise (Isaac) and the destiny of Abraham was unlocked and revealed. When Abraham allowed his identity to be merged with God, he was able to be what God created him to be and he left a legacy that is still talked about today. The name *"Isaac"* by the way, means *"laughter."* This is the product of finding one's true identity. It produces life satisfaction.

Matthew 10:38-40 "And he who does not take his cross and follow after Me is not worthy of Me. "He who has found his life will lose it, and he who has lost his life for My sake will find it. He who receives you receives Me, and he who receives Me receives Him who sent Me.

This is another picture of going from a position of individualism to a position of identity; from separation to mergence. He who loses his individualism and merges with Christ will find the true purpose for which they were created and will be empowered to emerge a new identity. Being born again positions you to begin the process that produces identity. When you were born-again, the Spirit of God merged with your spirit. You were positioned to begin operating from your true identity.

When we allow the disposition of Jesus to merge with us, we began to have HIS set ways acting through us. This requires your participation. Losing your life for His sake and taking up your cross to follow Him, involves being discipled. We give up our individual to become identified with Christ that we might accomplish in life that for which He has created us. In short, you will never know who you were created to be until you submit to the process of being a disciple of Jesus. Jesus first became identified with us before He asks us to be identified with Him.

> **Philippians 2:6-7** *who, although He existed in the form of God, did not regard equality with God a thing to be grasped, but emptied Himself, taking the form of a bond-servant, and being made in the likeness of men.*

How do we know that being discipled will perform the action of identifying us and our destinies? It is the process that God designed for all people to have access to in order to develop maturity or to be completed. What does it mean to be completed?

> **Galatians 4:19** *My children, with whom I am again in labor until Christ is formed in you—*

There is the idea found in the maturity of the saints that Jesus is being formed in us. This needs to be addressed and explored. The very statement *"...until Christ is formed in you"* suggests that it is a process that takes time to complete. We do not get saved and then suddenly we are ready to complete our destined journey. There is a time of preparation that must take place first. That begs the question, *"What is this preparation?"*

> **Ephesians 4:11-15** *And He gave some as apostles, and some as prophets, and some as evangelists, and some as pastors and teachers, for the equipping of the saints for the work of service, to the building up of the body of Christ; until we all attain to the unity of the faith, and of the knowledge of the Son of God,* ***to a mature man, to the measure of the stature which belongs to the fullness of Christ.*** *As a result, we are no longer to be children, tossed here and there by waves and carried about by every wind of doctrine, by the trickery of men, by craftiness in deceitful scheming; but speaking the truth in love, we are to* ***grow up in all aspects into Him who is the head, even Christ,***

Here we have the same language. The revelation then is that if we are to find our true identity and discover our true purpose, we must go through the discipleship process. There is something about going through that process that opens up to us the understanding and knowledge of who we really are and answers that nagging question that we have lived with our entire lives—*"Who am I?"* The key is discipleship and it is the very thing that Satan has stolen from the Church so that very few actually do enter in. Why is discipleship the key that unlocks my identity and destiny?

> **I Corinthians 2:16** *For who has known the mind of the Lord, that he will instruct Him? But we have the mind of Christ.*

The process of unfolding our destinies is to have Christ's disposition formed in us. The way that Christ is formed in us is by the equipping ministries of the five fold ministry.

> **Romans 8:29** *For those whom He foreknew, He also predestined to become conformed to the image of His Son, so that He would be the firstborn among many brethren;*

Being conformed into His disposition frees us to love one another as we see Him in us and in each other. This creates the atmosphere where we can merge with one another as one family. We become the family of God and we become brothers and sisters. As brothers and sisters we look out for each other, we protect each other, we instruct each other, and we love each other. God is glorified because we are in one accord; we are singing the same song with our lives no matter what part of the globe we are from because each of us has Christ formed in us!

> **Romans 12:4-5** *For just as we have many members in one body and all the members do not have the same function, so we, who are many, are one body in Christ, and individually members one of another.*

Therefore, George Bernard Shaw had it wrong on both fronts. In order to find our life we must lose individuality. If we create ourselves, we isolate and separate. The message of the world is to become like them and the message of Christ, is to have Christ formed in you—if—and this is a monumental if—you allow Christ to be formed in you by submitting to discipleship.

The Glory of God is Shriveling

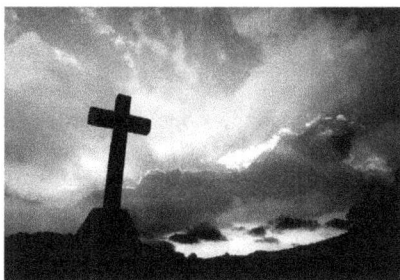

Chapter Seven

The subject of the glory of God is one that is not discussed much these days. At least I do not hear much that is said concerning it other than the obvious mention of it when the situation dictates. Nevertheless, I think it bears more attention because it is often thought of as something that exists in the nature of God and does not need much explanation.

There is much more to the glory of God than what most of us know. In fact, as Christians we participate in God's glory. What brought me to this subject in the first place is something that the Holy Spirit whispered to my heart; He said, *"The glory of God is shriveling in the earth."*

At the time I did not even understand the whole extent of what He said. Therefore, as I have done many times before, I cracked open the Bible and started to study the glory of God. I have found a number of different words that are translated to our English word *"glory,"* but only one Greek word that is translated the *"glory of God."* Let us look at what these words mean and see if we can define the glory of God as something concrete to us as humans.

What is Glory?

Before we look at the original words, let us look at what the English dictionary says glory is.

Definition – Glory

> *Glory n., pl.* ***glories****. 1. Great honor, praise, or distinction accorded by common consent; renown. 2. Something conferring honor or renown. 3. A highly praiseworthy asset: Your hair is your crowning glory. 4. Adoration, praise, and thanksgiving offered in worship. 5. Majestic beauty and splendor; resplendence: The sun set in a blaze of glory.*

From this, we see that our English word *"glory"* means great honor or praise. Now let us look at the Hebrew version of it.

> The Hebrew word is **kabod** and it means, *"heaviness."*

The root Hebrew word for *"glory"* is *"weighty."* Glory is a spiritual component of God that has great weight. The picture is that of a person of great wealth, thus the weight of gold that they have.

> The Greek word is **doxa** and it means, *"good opinion, judgment, view, estimate, splendor, brightness, magnificence, excellence, preeminenence, dignity, grace, and majesty."*

I want you to keep these words in your mind as we proceed: *good opinion, brightness, majesty, honor, worship, magnificence, excellence, dignity, and grace.* These are the descriptors used to describe God's glory.

Some of my favorite verses that provide us with a description of Jesus, are the first few verses of Hebrews. I am still nagged by the question, *"How could God's glory be shriveling?"* After all, He is God; He can show the earth whatever He wants.

> **Hebrews 1:1-4** *In the past God spoke to our forefathers through the prophets at many times and in various ways, but in these last days he has spoken to us by his Son, whom he appointed heir of all things, and through whom he made the universe.* **The Son is the radiance of God's glory and the exact representation of his being,** *sustaining all things by his powerful word. After he had provided purification for sins, he sat down at the right hand of the Majesty in heaven. So he became as much superior to the angels as the name he has inherited is superior to theirs.*

What a beautiful description of Jesus this is! We see that He is the radiance of God's glory. That means He reflects all those attributes of glory to us. Do you remember those words I asked you to remember? *(good opinion, brightness, majesty, honor, worship, magnificence, excellence, dignity and grace)* Jesus expressed, is expressing, and will express to us the very glory of God. How is this possible? It was evidenced by what He did while He was among us. Everything Jesus said and did brought glory to God. He reflected exactly the essence of who God is.

Intensity

We get the sense that glory is attached to the intensity of light. One of the many places this is seen is:

> *Acts 22:11 (KJV) And when I could not see for the* **glory** *of that light, being led by the hand of them that were with me, I came into Damascus.*

> *Acts 22:11 "But since I could not see because of the* **brightness** *of that light, I was led by the hand by those who were with me, and came into Damascus.*

I included this verse in two different translations so you can see that the word glory, as used by the King James Version, is the same word that other versions translate as brightness, or brilliance. Yet the same Greek word *(doxa)*, is used for the glory of God. This gives us the indication that glory is the brightness, or intensity of the light. It would not make sense to say *"the good opinion of the light."* Imagine for a moment that a candle has one glory or brightness, and a light bulb has a different glory or brightness.

> *I Corinthians 15:41-44 There is one glory of the sun, and another glory of the moon, and another glory of the stars; for star differs from star in glory. So is it with the resurrection of the dead. What is sown is perishable, what is raised is imperishable. It is sown in dishonor, it is raised in glory. It is sown in weakness, it is raised in power. It is sown a physical body, it is raised a spiritual body. If there is a physical body, there is also a spiritual body.*

Therefore, what we can learn from this passage is that our lives, after we are resurrected, will declare the glory of God in a greater aspect then we can now. In other words, we will be brighter individuals; we will shine the awesome love and character of our Creator. **The other thing revealed here is that there are different intensities to glory.** Moreover, it is this event that causes the sons of God to be revealed.

> ***Romans 8:19*** *For the anxious longing of the creation waits eagerly for the **revealing of the sons of God.***

> ***Romans 8:22-23*** *For we know that the whole creation groans and suffers the pains of childbirth together until now. And not only this, but also we ourselves, having the first fruits of the Spirit, even we ourselves groan within ourselves, waiting eagerly for **our adoption as sons**, the redemption of our body.*

In Him we move, breathe, and have our being. In Him today we can experience joy, peace, longsuffering, love, kindness, gentleness, patience, meekness, and faith; also, we experience these in supernatural quantities. In our natural state, we experience these things in part, but in the hereafter, we experience them in perfection.

Therefore, in our resurrected state we could say that we will be brighter or more intense than we are now. In other words, we will be revealed as more glorious at that time than we are now. What about now? What types of glory if any, do we show now?

> ***II Corinthians 3:6-8*** *He has made us competent as ministers of a new covenant—not of the letter but of*

*the Spirit; for **the letter kills**, but the Spirit gives
life. 7 Now if the ministry that brought death, which
was engraved in letters on stone, **came with glory**,
so that the Israelites could not look steadily at the
face of Moses because of its glory, fading though it
was, 8 will not the ministry of the Spirit be even
more glorious?*

We know from the Old Testament that the giving of the commandments meant death to us. Why? Because of the sin nature we inherited from Adam, no single human would ever keep the commandments. Consequently, the law meant certain death to us. That is why Paul said, *"the letter kills"* for he was speaking of the commandments.

The line of thought that Paul was using here, is if the Law, which meant certain death for us, was glorious then what of it now? When Moses returned from having received the Law from God, the Bible says that his face radiated God's glory.

> ***Exodus 34:29-31*** *When Moses came down from
> Mount Sinai with the two tablets of the Testimony in
> his hands, he was not aware that his face was
> radiant **because** he had spoken with the LORD.
> When Aaron and all the Israelites saw Moses, his
> face was radiant, and they were afraid to come near
> him. But Moses called to them; so Aaron and all the
> leaders of the community came back to him, and he
> spoke to them.*

Paul calls the radiance that Moses exhibited *"glory"* (II Corinthians 3:7). That which meant certain death was glorious, so much so that Moses' face was lit up with the glory of God. So how much more glorious is that which means certain life to us? Of course, I am speaking of the ministry of the Holy Spirit. How much more glorious is our freedom from the Law; how much more glorious is our salvation from dead works; how much more glorious is our forgiveness from sin; how much more glorious is our position in God?

> *II Corinthians 3:9 If the ministry that condemns men is glorious, how much more glorious is the ministry that brings righteousness!*

The giving of the Law instantly condemned the entire human race to death, and it was called glorious! Now I have been made righteous, even given the righteousness of God, and oh how much more glorious this is!

> *II Corinthians 3:10 For what was glorious has no glory now in comparison with the surpassing glory.*

Hence, in comparing the giving of the Law and the giving of grace, Paul is saying that the Law has no glory at all in comparison. We know that it did have glory, however, as demonstrated with how Moses' face shown with the glory of God. Yet, in comparison, it was not at all glorious when side by side with the Good News. That is how huge the gap is between a belief that demands animal sacrifice and a gospel that gives perfection.

It is so far removed from the former that it cannot even be compared to it. In order for a comparison to take place, there must be at least a measurable quantity in both objects of what is being compared. Grace is so much more glorious than animal sacrifices that when held side by side, it appears that the works of the Law have no brightness at all.

II Corinthians 3:11 And if what was fading away came with glory, how much greater is the glory of that which lasts!

The brightness of Moses' face was fading away, **but the brightness of grace in our lives is forever.** Paul is saying that the fading away of the brightness of Moses' face is actually the fading of God's glory concerning the Law and the system of sacrifice.

We have a High Priest, Jesus the Christ, Who provided the way for every man and woman to enter into His gates of glory through His shed blood on Calvary. How can we deny such a glorious gift?

II Corinthians 3:12-13 Therefore, since we have such a hope, we are very bold. We are not like Moses, who would put a veil over his face to keep the Israelites from gazing at it while the radiance was fading away.

Moses put a veil over his face to keep those Israelites from noticing that the glory was fading away. This has to be one of the most misquoted Scriptures in the Bible. I have heard people say that the veil was used because Moses' face was too bright to be looked upon. This is not what Paul is saying. Paul says that we are not like Moses, who would put a veil over his face to keep them from seeing it fade away. Therefore, we are very bold in our proclamation of the Good News; we do not shrink away from the message of the Gospel.

II Corinthians 3:14-15 But their minds were made dull, for to this day the same veil remains when the old covenant is read. It has not been removed,

*because only in Christ is it taken away. Even to this
day when Moses is read, a veil covers their hearts.*

I used to read this and think of the veil as something that kept
them from seeing the truth. Now I read it in the context of what
was the reason for Moses wearing it. I see that it is not to keep
something outside from getting in, but to keep something on the
inside from getting out. The glory is fading away for those who
wear this veil; the glory of God is fading from their lives. Their
minds are dull. Only Christ can take away the veil so that God's
glory could be shown in us without fading away.

> *II Corinthians 3:16-18 But whenever anyone turns
> to the Lord, the veil is taken away. Now the Lord is
> the Spirit, and where the Spirit of the Lord is, there
> is freedom. And we, who with unveiled faces all
> reflect the Lord's glory, **are being transformed into
> his likeness with ever-increasing glory**, which
> comes from the Lord, who is the Spirit.*

"And we, who with unveiled faces..." Who is that? It is those
who have allowed the Lord to save their life through the blood
atonement of the cross by simply believing in Him. *"...all reflect
the Lord's glory..."* Who reflects the Lord's glory? It is those with
unveiled faces. Those who are His and have unveiled faces are
reflections of God's glory. Now we return to what the Spirit said to
me. *"My glory is shriveling in the earth."* Now this is starting to
make sense. What does shriveling actually mean?

Definition – Shrivel

> **shriv·el 1.** *To become or make shrunken and
> wrinkled, often by drying: Leaves die, fall, and*

shrivel. The heat shriveled the unwatered seedlings.
2. To lose or cause to lose vitality or intensity: *My*
enthusiasm shriveled as the project wore on.
Inflation shriveled the buying power of the dollar. **3.**
To become or make much less or smaller; dwindle.

"To lose or cause to lose vitality or intensity." Now I am
looking at this in the realm of the intensity of light. God's glory is
losing its intensity in the lives of His creation. Its brightness is
fading.

"...are being transformed into His likeness with ever-
increasing glory..." What would stop this from happening in the
Christian's life? It would diminish when we are unwilling to take
the path that Jesus has given us to walk. In other words, **we deny**
our destiny and the purpose for which we are called. God's
glory is shriveling because we are not producing what God
intended us to produce.

"...ever-increasing glory, which comes from the Lord, who is
the Spirit." Ever-increasing glory comes from God; it does not
come from man.

Bearing Fruit

> **John 15:5** *"I am the vine, you are the branches; he*
> *who abides in Me, and I in him, he bears much*
> *fruit; **for apart from Me you can do nothing.***

So what is abiding in the Vine? Let us look at nature to get the
answer. A branch that is connected to the root is fed by that root.
The root gives nourishment to the branches, and the branches bring
glory to the root. If the branch is cut off, then it withers and dies,

and has no more life. So it is with Christ and us, everything we do comes from the Vine, and we show the Vine's glory when we are abiding in Him and are bearing fruit.

When we go off on our own to do what we think is right, then we cease to produce fruit from the vine; we are cut off and begin to wither and die spiritually and sometimes even physically. Abiding in the Vine is surrendering your life to the will of the Vine in order that the Vine may cause you to **produce the fruit** that He desires. What is required from you is your obedience to His will. That is abiding in the Vine. If you will remember, I showed earlier the similarity between the brightness of light and glory. Let us now see another connection.

> **John 15:8** *My true disciples produce much fruit. This brings great glory to my Father.*

As disciples of Christ, we are supposed to produce much fruit. We cannot produce any fruit on our own though for it takes an act of God to do so. Only those who are true disciples produce much fruit.

> **Matthew 5:14** *"You are the light of the world. A city set on a hill cannot be hidden.*

We who are abiding in the Vine are the light of the whole world…if we are walking out our destinies. If we are the light of the world, then what is our brightness? Are you allowing God to form you into His likeness?

> **Matthew 5:15** *"Nor do men light a lamp, and put it under the peck-measure, but on the lampstand; and it gives light to all who are in the house.*

The purpose of God putting His light in us is so that the rest of the world would see His glory and want to partake of it as well. This is the purpose of your existence in Christ, to reveal His glory to a world that is lost and on a course of destruction.

> **Matthew 5:16** *"Let your light shine before men in such a way that they may **see your good works**, and **glorify** your Father who is in heaven.*

"Let your light shine…" What is the glory of your light; what is its brightness? We see that we are to show forth God's glory. We see that the glory of God in our lives is bearing good fruit. We see that bearing good fruit is doing good works. We see that doing good works can only be accomplished by abiding in the Vine.

So why is the glory of God shriveling? **It is happening because we who are His are not doing the works that He has called us to do.** If we are not willing to follow the Vine's direction for our discipleship, we will never come into the glory God has ordained for us. Moreover, if we do not come into the glory of God, we will not have anything to show the world.

We live in a society where it is acceptable to curse the name of Jesus, but to speak of Him in honor makes you seem strange and it is unacceptable as normal social behavior. Why should we shrink from our Lord and not speak of His name in honor? Are we to listen to men and do what they say, or are we to listen to God and do what He says? We need to proclaim our faith boldly without fear of offence. If we want to spare others for fear of offending them because of the name of Christ, then we offend Christ.

God did not make His light available to you so that you could hide or so that the world could not see what was in you. He put His light in you so that you would show others this light. For this light is life and love for a dying human race. To hide God's glory from this human race is to damn them to hell, all because we are unwilling to submit to the process of being equipped and prepared for God's use, purpose, and fulfillment for our lives.

Discipleship

John 17:4 "*I glorified You on the earth, having accomplished the work which You have given Me to do.*

Jesus always sets the pattern for us. Here He reveals that He glorified the Father by **accomplishing the work that He had given Jesus to do.** How then do you glorify the Father?

John 17:6-10 "*I have manifested Your name to the men whom You gave Me out of the world; they were Yours and You gave them to Me, and they have kept Your word. Now they have come to know that everything You have given Me is from You;* **for the words which You gave Me I have given to them;** *and they received them and truly understood that I came forth from You, and they believed that You sent Me. I ask on their behalf; I do not ask on behalf of the world, but of those whom You have given Me; for they are Yours; and all things that are Mine are Yours, and Yours are Mine; and* **I have been glorified in them.**

Jesus gave His disciples the Word of God. In other words, He discipled them. This discipling is the process that brings us to the place where we are able to glorify Jesus. For the most part, the Church has abandoned discipleship. We allow the glory of God to shrivel when we are not willing to continue this discipleship process or we walk away from being discipled.

As a Christian, you have a great treasure inside you, and this treasure is your purpose and destiny. If you do not live it, you will not bring glory to God. You cannot live it unless you have followed the process of discipleship. So let your light shine! Let God make it brighter and brighter!

> *II Corinthians 3:18 But we all, with unveiled face, beholding as in a mirror the glory of the Lord, are being transformed into the same image from glory to glory, just as from the Lord, the Spirit.*

Abide in the Vine so that you would do the works of your Father. Thank Him always for the life that beats within you because of what He has done on the cross.

Do you remember those words I told you to remember? Our lives should be such that they bring a good opinion, brightness, majesty, honor, worship, magnificence, excellence, dignity, and grace to our Lord. Does your life bring these things to God? Have you submitted to the process of discipleship whereby you are transformed into the image of Christ?

How Can I Be More Brilliant?

Chapter Eight

I n the previous chapter we found that we as Christians are to exhibit the glory of God in our lives. We also saw that glory could be compared to the brilliance of light. We found that this brilliance or glory fades in us when we go from grace to works to be justified. In addition, we are unable to increase our brilliance because we try to bypass the process that God established for maturity, i.e., discipleship.

If we are under the grace of God and submitted to discipleship, some things can still slow us down or stop us. What I want to discuss in this chapter are some of the things that can stop us in becoming more brilliant. What I mean by brilliance is not intellectual acuteness, although that is a benefit of it, but the brightness of God's glory in our lives.

In previous chapters, I discussed how abiding in the Vine (Jesus) allows us to produce fruit. We also saw that God's glory is displayed in our lives through us by bearing fruit. We also learned that fruit is synonymous with doing what God has called you to do, or good works. If we do produce fruit then the Father will prune us so that we may produce more fruit. It is this pruning process that I want to look at now.

The Pruning Process

> **John 15:1-2** *"I am the true vine, and My Father is the vinedresser. Every branch in Me that does not bear fruit, He takes away; and every branch that bears fruit, He prunes it, that it may bear more fruit."*

I researched the process of *"pruning"* and what I found was an interesting parallel with life. Pruning results in the removal of parts of woody plants, usually branches or branch tips, to **relieve the burden** on the remaining parts of the plant. Pruning is also for **cutting out diseased or broken parts**, to **increase the quantity and quality of flowers or fruits**, to **train individual parts to positions structurally favorable to the health of the plant, or to shape the plant into some artificial form.**

In addition, the action of wind, excessive fruit loads, and ice or snow, produces a natural pruning. Such natural pruning frequently leaves stubs or slowly healing wounds that are susceptible to decay and disease. The hollows that result provide feeding areas, nesting sites, and shelter for arboreal animals. Artificial pruning prevents decay and promotes quick healing of wounds.

In short, effective purposeful pruning relieves burdens, removes disease or broken parts, trains and shapes to increase the quantity and quality of the fruit, and brings health to the plant. We also see that natural pruning is detrimental to the growth of the plant and opens it up to disease.

Let us see if we can apply this to our lives. Notice that the Vinedresser is God the Father. Jesus is the Vine and we are the branches. The Father wants to make your life more fruitful. **He wants to heal you of the effects of natural pruning.** He wants to make you grow and He wants to shape you.

Bearing fruit are the works that we as Christians do. It is not just those things we do occasionally, but also those things we do often. It is not just what we do openly, but what we do in private when no one is looking. It is not just those things that we think God would take notice of, but also those things we do on a daily basis that show we are led by a code of right and wrong.

What about the branches that are not bearing fruit and yet they are in the Vine? Notice that the Vine does not force the branches to bear fruit, and neither will the Vinedresser. This is where abiding must take place. Abiding means that I am allowing the vine to nourish me and I am allowing the Vinedresser to prune me.

The Vine only gives the branches *POWER* to produce fruit, and the Vine Dresser only gives the branches the best *ENVIRONMENT* to bear fruit. The fruit bearing is actually up to us, the branches. We have the power from Jesus and the favorable environment from the Father to do so. It is up to our will to choose to bear fruit.

There is a bit of an oxymoron in this as well. Even though it is up to us as Christians to bear fruit, we are also incapable of bearing fruit. It is only through merging yourself with your Creator that you are able to bear fruit. Bearing fruit is a partnership of the utmost proportions with God.

By looking at the causes of bearing little fruit, we can understand how to bear much fruit. Now I do not want you to misunderstand me here. I am not saying that it is SOLELY up to you to do works. What I am saying is you have a part in the process.

Remember that Jesus said, *"You can do NOTHING without me."* Nevertheless, this does not mean that we do not have a part. It is just that we cannot do it without Him, but we are to do and doing means an act of our individual will. My part is to submit to the process of His pruning. That is His making me into a vessel that can bear fruit.

> *II Corinthians 4:7 But this precious treasure-this light and power that now shine within us-is held in perishable containers, that is, in our weak bodies. So everyone can see that our glorious power is from God and is not our own.*

We must never lose sight of the fact that God's glorious brilliance is contained in perishable containers. If we have an expectation of perfection, we will be terribly disappointed. If we understand that God chooses to use faulty containers then we can get the focus off our container and equally off other's containers and concentrate on the work of bearing fruit.

If we do not DO, then all the equipping, all of the preparation, all of the desire is for nothing! It produced no fruit! We have to DO when God equips and sends us to DO! If you will not, God will allow trials and tribulations to fall upon you until you come to the place through suffering where you are rid of SELF! This pruning process causes you to start working or bearing fruit.

God will continue to prune you until you come to that place where you can experience life abundant. This is what trials are for, to rid you of the things that keep you from entering into God's rest and experiencing the true and abundant life. But when you want to do your OWN thing, God will not stop you for you possess free will, but He will influence you through a life of hardship till you come to the place where you say, *"Yes Lord,"* and you DO!

I have found in my walk with God that I can think that I have surrendered all, but in reality, I have areas that are still in a state of my control. I have found that I have had baggage that I am not conscious of without a strong internal look into my soul. In order to be the best that I can be, I must get to a place where I am ALL His. Note that God's pruning is often to correct or heal the effects of natural pruning. The wind from storms will produce wounds that produce scars.

These scars become strong high walls of a fortress where I am protecting something that God wants to release. These walls are defense mechanisms that protect areas in my life where I feel vulnerable. Walls can keep me from receiving the fullness of God's truth. If I cannot receive the fullness of God's truth, I am stopped from displaying the fullness of the glory of that truth.

Natural Pruning

In nature, there is a natural pruning from the wind and the storms. In the lives of humans, there are pressures (winds) and events (storms) that shape our lives in ways that open us up to distress. I am talking about emotional distress. These distresses leave wounds that heal slowly and open us up to other diseases.

What is a Wall?

A wall is an **area of hurt** in your life that for various reasons you have built a wall around to protect it. There are wounds that we suffer that cause us to erect a stronghold that is actually a survival mechanism. That stronghold also keeps us from being healed. You become vulnerable through the wound; hence, you built the wall to protect your vulnerability. You cannot come to healing until you expose the wound and allow God to process healing in you.

Every wall or stronghold also becomes a filter. A filter is a particular way of thinking based upon a trauma experienced by you. Because the wound becomes a stronghold, which then becomes a filter, every bit of information is filtered through that stronghold which can cause us to misunderstand or misinterpret what others are saying or doing. Every wall or stronghold is also a way of believing. Walls are nothing more than beliefs and these beliefs filter information. The original information that is in its pure form (that is the full intent and purpose of that information), is then altered to form it into what you believe.

Filtering everything someone says or does through this belief has the effect of changing information you hear. However, the wall is not based in truth, but it is based in experience and that experience created the environment that would give rise to a lie. It is a lie that you swallowed and digested until it became truth to you. This wall affects your relationship with God and individuals. It also diminishes God's glory in your life. There are things in all of our lives that keep us from receiving the fullness of God's truth!

Natural pruning is usually harmful. Although, if we allow God to prune us, (artificial pruning) He can heal these areas and bring restoration. Not only can He bring restoration, but He can make that place of vulnerability a strong place where it becomes an ability to minister to others in that same area.

Notice the love of God. If we are bearing a little fruit, He comes along, inspects us, and finds areas that are preventing us from bearing more fruit. Then He begins the pruning process to bring healing into these areas so that we are able to receive more truth and as a result bear more fruit. What a loving Father He is!

Pressures (Wind)

Wind represents those things that were or are constant in your life. They are not things that come and go in a short time period. They are long-term conditions that have wounded us. The consistency of the wind brings to bear a pressure that is constant and has an effect over time that can mount and increase with time. As we go through some of these things, the effects that we list are not all inclusive. There are a myriad of things that can issue out of wounds.

1. Poverty

    Poverty is a pressure that molds people in different ways.

    - It can shape us into fatalism where we think nothing good will ever happen. When we begin to believe that we are destined to lack, we enter into depression. So we prepare ourselves never to expect anything but more of the same. This belief structure forfeits faith in God Who seeks to prosper His children.

    - It can shape us into hording. Because we believe that we will always be without, we are unable to give because we see giving as bringing more poverty rather than prosperity. God said that if we give, He would give back in abundance. If we horde we become like those Israelites who would take more manna then they needed and God caused it to spoil as a result and the worms ate it.

- It can shape us into stealing. Because we believe that we will never have, we may become thieves. We are set up psychologically to believe that the only way we will survive is to take from others. Yet in reality thievery always brings on poverty. God says that He will take from those who steal.

- It can shape us into class warfare and despising the rich. Because we believe that we will never have or that we can never get, we are set up to despise those that do have. This causes us to treat them poorly or to speak of them poorly. In doing this, we are despising our own prosperity, but we never think of it that way.

- It can shape us into despising God. When we believe that our plight is because of God, we will not trust God and we will not enter into the relationship that God wants with us. We may see God as the source of our poverty. God wants to bless His children but if we believe in God making us poor, then we are unable to receive from Him, which only perpetuates our poverty.

2. Substance Abuse Environment

Growing up in a household where there is substance abuse is a constant pressure that has a measurable effect on the person. It should be noted, however, that there are different levels concerning this environment and this should be taken into consideration when reading some of the effects.

- It can shape us into acceptance of immorality. One very damaging effect of growing up in a home where substance abuse is common is that the use of the substance is normalized or at the very least, it is made permissible by the parents. The normalization of this environment opens the gate to the use of these substances in the lives of the children.

- It can shape us into an entitlement mentality. Substance abuse often produces an entitlement mentality where people think that others should take care of them or provide for them. When a person has an entitlement mentality, they cannot bring themselves to trust in the Lord. They have the expectation that humanity owes it to them to care for them.

- It can shape us to be selfish. Because those who are substance abusers often display frequent moments of selfishness, that environment can be a learned behavior for children. Substance abusers are almost always models of selfishness.

3. Sexual Abuse Environment

- It can shape us to have a constant sense of abandonment. Because those whom we trusted did these things, we can feel abandoned throughout life. That abandonment can often be directed toward God. This causes the person to be unable to trust in God because they feel He will abandon them. Yet Jesus said that He would never leave us.

- It can shape a person to live in fear. Because sexual abuse is an act of violence, the victim can feel a sense of fear even when they are in a safe environment. God wants us to be free of fear and to place all of our trust in Him. However, this wall will not allow it. Fear has torment. Faith has peace.

4. Emotional Abuse Environment

An emotional abuse environment can be devastating.

- It can shape a person to have unsubstantiated negative beliefs about themselves. For instance, if through your life you have been told that you are worthless, ugly, stupid, dumb, an idiot, etc., you may have an area in your life that causes you to reinforce this belief or to build an area that is impenetrable when it comes to things attributed to your self worth. Many that are treated this way by those they give the most trust, begin to believe that their abusers were right. This is a wall.

- This belief then becomes a filter in your mind, so that everything someone says is filtered through this belief. If this filter is one of low self-esteem, then everything that is said or done is looked upon with great scrutiny to determine if there actually are things that are attacking your character thereby reinforcing the belief that you are no good. In fact, it causes you to misinterpret or change what others say and do.

- If you hold the belief that you are worthless, and God says you are of great price, you cannot receive the fullness of that truth because of the wall. You will try, but you just seem not to be able to believe that God really thinks that you are valuable. The reason is that it disagrees with what you believe.

- Now that you have swallowed the lie that you are worthless, you begin to do things that will protect your idea of your own esteem. This defense mechanism will keep you from being in a situation whereby others can build you up. This will lead to more depression and the vicious cycle continues, even to the point of complete destruction of your life. Satan is the one that wants you to continue to believe you are worthless.

- This can shape a person to feel a need to control. It can cause a fear of the lack of control over one's life. This wall is built upon a section of your life where another forcibly controlled and manipulated you. Having experienced this, one builds a wall around giving control of your life to another. Every belief that you have becomes a filter to every outside sense that you have. The wall or beliefs in your heart will filter every bit of information that comes to you, no matter what sense it comes through. This causes the truth to be distorted, warped, weak, ineffective, and even destructive.

- The person that fears losing control will try to control everything, leaving nothing to chance, so they will not find themselves ever in a place where another human being can control them. Can you see how this affects our lives with God? It is imperative that we give God control in order that we might do His works. However, because you have a wall that is protecting an area in your life, in this case control, then the Spirit is ineffective because we cannot give Him control. You want to give Him total control, but you cannot. You try, but find that you are ineffective.

Events (Storms)

Many events happen to humanity. Events are different from pressures in that they are sudden and are temporary. Pressures last a long time whereas storms are short lived. The effect of either can be just as destructive. In our list of events, we cannot even begin to catalog them all. We will just list some that are current to our time and our culture.

1. Adultery

- You may find that you have a wall of mistrust. This wall is caused by those that are in your inner circle of relationship saying one thing and doing another. This causes you to build a wall of mistrust of others regardless of how trustworthy they are, including God. Do you find that you cannot totally trust God in everything He says? You may have erected a wall of mistrust.

Before I go any further, I want to say this. These walls are often raised as defense mechanisms and are a natural result of how you were treated. What I mean by this is oftentimes we cannot stop the wall from erecting itself as a natural way of defending ourselves. Some walls like low self-esteem are self-destructing, but again these things come about because of how we are treated.

- Another wall that is erected in one's life is hate. When those that are in your inner circle treat you with hate, you may erect a wall of hate toward others. When you are the one that is being mistreated, you may perceive yourself as being weak, and the one that is doing the mistreatment you may perceive as being strong. So in order to go from being weak and vulnerable to being strong, one mimics what they perceive as strong so that they will be in power instead of being the powerless one.

This is something that you often see in those abused by parents or loved ones. They learned a system of hate. They learned that those that do the hating get what they want from those they hate through abuse. What comes out of this is a wall of control. The one that hates is perceived as being in control and those being hated as being out of control. This will keep you from submitting to God's power for this would make you powerless in your own perception, when in reality it makes us powerful when we partner with and submit to God.

2. Death

- The death of a loved one can erect a wall of depression. Grieving is natural, but some take grieving all the way to depression. When this is done, there is a belief that things will never become normal again. That belief will keep one under the bondage of depression. It does not make room for God's healing touch. The Bible states, *"Blessed are they that mourn, for they shall be comforted."*

- It can erect a wall of loneliness. When one believes that they will now be alone for the rest of their lives, loneliness is accepted as the norm. Loneliness leads again to depression.

Do you think that Satan is aware of your walls? Do you think that he will exploit that weakness to his benefit and your destruction? You bet he will! All of the time you were susceptible to the winds and storms of life, Satan was trying to reinforce those lies by making suggestions to your mind. If you want your life to be what God intended, and if you want to experience the fullness of God's truth, and if you want to experience God's abundant life, then you must rid yourself of these filters and lies.

There are also combinations of walls that cause problems. If we look at jealousy, we see there is a wall of mistrust and a wall of control involved. There are many different combinations at work, but they all have the same effect. They keep us from being as brilliant as God wants us to be.

These walls are also areas in our lives that Satan has power and influence over because we are in agreement with Satan and out of agreement with God. God has not been given permission to tear down those walls to get to these sore spots to heal you. The devil only has as much power as you hand to him. That is why he has to use deception and events to plant untruths to gain power.

> **Luke 10:19** *And I have given you authority over all the power of the enemy, and you can walk among snakes and scorpions and crush them. Nothing will injure you.*

We are not to be ships tossed to and fro at the enemy's every whim. We are, however, tossed to and fro as a result of our own belief structure that causes us to open a door for Satan to torment us. The reason is that we cannot receive from God into our walled in areas because inside those walls we are out of agreement with what God has already said. These walls are areas that we have erected to protect a way of thinking. This way of thinking is contrary to what God thinks.

I have seen many people that hurt so much and cannot seem to get past the hurt. They can, God has given them the keys to the kingdom, but we only receive where we unlock. If we do not take those keys and unlock the gates to those strongholds, we will not receive. God has so much for you as an individual, you are of great price, and you are called according to His purpose.

Getting Set Free

How do we get rid of the fortified walls in our lives?

> *II Corinthians 10:4-5 (KJV) For the weapons of our warfare are not carnal but mighty in God for pulling down strongholds, casting down arguments and every high thing that exalts itself against the knowledge of God, bringing every thought into captivity to the obedience of Christ,*

Our weaponry is not with or of the flesh; we cannot defeat strongholds with our own ability. We defeat them with divinely powerful weapons. Look at the first part of verse five. What argument exalts itself against God's knowledge? When you think of yourself as unworthy, that is in direct opposition to what God thinks.

This is an argument that exalts itself against the knowledge of God. God thinks one way and you, because of the stronghold you erected, think another way. Anything that is contrary to the absolute truth delivered to us by God is an argument that exalts itself against the knowledge of God. It is us humans declaring that we know better than God does, that we are somehow wiser than God is.

The weapons of our warfare bring into captivity every thought to the obedience of Christ, not our own will power. We know that we have the sword of the Spirit that is the Word of God. When you look in the Word of God and see a principle or truth, you can stand on that as absolute truth. Everything that is against that truth is a lie.

Binding and Losing

> **Matthew 16:19** *"I will give you the keys of the kingdom of heaven; and whatever you shall bind on earth shall be bound in heaven, and whatever you shall loose on earth shall be loosed in heaven."*

> **Matthew 18:18-20** *"Truly I say to you, whatever you shall bind on earth shall be bound in heaven; and whatever you loose on earth shall be loosed in heaven. "Again I say to you, that if two of you agree on earth about anything that they may ask, it shall be done for them by My Father who is in heaven. "For where two or three have gathered together in My name, there I am in their midst."*

What do keys do? They lock or bind, and they unlock or loose. Keys denote control or power. If you look on your key ring, you can find the things that you have control of. No one goes to your car and drives away except a thief or someone that you gave permission. You retain control over your car because you have the keys that unlock the doors; you have the keys to start the car. You are in control of your car. We also have spiritual keys. What do they control, what do they unlock, and what do they lock?

Now since these keys are called the *"keys of the kingdom of heaven,"* they must unlock and lock things from the kingdom of heaven. They must bring to us kingdom living on earth. Does the Word point to this also?

Matthew 3:2 *"Repent, for the kingdom of heaven is at hand."*

John the Baptist arrived at the Jordan River saying that the kingdom of heaven is a hand. In other words, it was there, it had arrived. What do we mean by kingdom of heaven? Every kingdom has a king or ruler; we know that the King of heaven is our God. We also know that Satan rules over the earth. We can see this by his offering to Jesus to give Him all of his kingdoms, if He would but worship him. The kingdom of heaven coming to the earth means that God's rule would now be extended and exerted upon earth.

Luke 11:20 *"But if I cast out demons by the finger of God, then the kingdom of God has come upon you*

In this verse, Jesus is showing us here that we can know that the kingdom is come upon us by the fact that He was displaying power over the ruler of this world. Moreover, if He, the King of kings, is displaying power over the ruler of this world then He must be King, and His kingdom has come to us.

Luke 17:20-21 *Now when He was asked by the Pharisees when the kingdom of God would come, He answered them and said, "The kingdom of God does not come with observation; "nor will they say, 'See here!' or 'See there!' For indeed, the kingdom of God is within you."*

The kingdom or rule of God is within us. It does not come with observation, that is, it is spiritual, not physical. If this is so, why do we have so much trouble giving Him rule over our lives? We have to remember that God created us with a free will. In His sovereignty God created us this way. In fact, He had to make us that way.

If God is love, He is incapable of making anything in His image that is incapable of love. Since love cannot exist in the environment of enslavement, we have to be created with free will. Since He did create us with free will, He will not force Himself into any part of our life that we do not invite Him. These areas are the walls that we discussed earlier.

In order to tear down these walls we must access the kingdom of heaven with the keys of the kingdom. We must unlock the gates of these strongholds and let God's kingdom come in to rule these areas of our life. We do this by making a conscious decision to let God into the areas that we have been so protective of.

First, we lock out the devil from influence in these areas or walls by coming out of agreement with his lies. Then we unlock that stronghold in our lives by coming into agreement with what God has said. The keys of the kingdom are actually God's Words. All of this is done without consideration of how we feel. In fact, doing this might cause some weeping and anxieties at first, for you are exposing areas of your life that you have protected for years. There are things that you hid away with lock and key because of the pain that is raised by dealing with them.

That is okay; you can and must trust God with these areas. This is not something that will be done once either. Your flesh, your emotional pain will try to erect a wall to defend that area of your life repeatedly until you come to the full knowledge of God's immutable truth. So be prepared to do this every time a thought comes up that reveals to you that you have erected that wall again.

Jesus defeated the devil with, *"it is written...."* God's Word is your mighty weapon against every thought that would exalt itself against the knowledge of God. God's Word is a solution to every problem that you have. When the devil tells you that you are worthless, you can say, *"Oh no I'm not, for it is written, 'For you have been bought with a price: therefore glorify God in your body.'"* What is the price He paid for you? That should reveal to you how much you are actually worth. Is the life of God in the flesh a worthy price?

God's Pruning

How can we express the fullness of God's love to others if we do not receive the fullness of God's love for ourselves? In order to express the full brilliance of God's truth, we must RECEIVE the full brilliance of God's truth! God prunes us that we may show more of His glory. We are going from glory to glory. He wants us to express His image in our lives that He might win more souls. He takes no pleasure in the destruction of the wicked. He would that no one perishes. He uses you and me to express His love and glory to a dying world that more would want to come to the light and experience it.

We cannot win souls without letting God shine in our lives. Remember, Jesus was the One who is the brightness of His glory and the express image of His person. This is God's goal for us as well. He wants us to shine His glory throughout the world. He called us the light of the world. We are the brightness of His glory.

> *John 17:20-23 "I pray for these followers, but I am also praying for all those who will believe in me because of their teaching. Father, I pray that they can be one. As you are in me and I am in you, I pray*

that they can also be one in us. Then the world will believe that you sent me. I have given these people the glory that you gave me so that they can be one, just as you and I are one. I will be in them and you will be in me so that they will be completely one. Then the world will know that you sent me and that you loved them just as much as you loved me.

Jesus left us to do more of the work that He did. He said that the works that He did, we will do also and greater works then these will we do. This means that we have for us the same Spirit that He has and as a result, we can do things according to that Spirit as He did. We can heal the sick, cast out devils, see into the hearts of men, walk in holiness, and do miracles, etc.

> **Galatians 3:13** *Christ redeemed us from the curse of the law by becoming a curse for us, for it is written: "Cursed is everyone who is hung on a tree."*

Our curse is broken; Christ took it when He died on the cross! We have been given the keys of the kingdom. We are not subject to the rule of Satan over this world. If you are not a Christian and have not applied the sacrifice of Christ to your life you are under the rule and reign of the devil. If you are a Christian, you have dominion over Satan. Greater is he that is in you than he that is in the world!

> **Ephesians 2:4-6** *But God, who is rich in mercy, because of His great love with which He loved us, even when we were dead in trespasses, made us alive together with Christ (by grace you have been saved), and raised us up together, and made us sit together in the heavenly places in Christ Jesus,*

We are partakers of God's kingdom! We are made to sit with Him in the heavenly places. We are not the defeated of the world; we have an inheritance that makes us neither proud nor haughty, for we were given a gift whereby we were made into adopted children of the living victorious God. Being not of haughty or proud spirit, we most humbly call to those our brothers and sisters that have not joined us yet—to come and partake of the forgiveness of God and become a beacon of His glory in the world.

We are not weaklings, we are kings and priests and we have power! The One that destroyed the works of the devil has given this power to us. If God destroyed the works of the devil, why then do we act as if the devil is so powerful? HE IS DEFEATED! Jesus our Lord and Christ defeated him by destroying his power. Jesus imparted the power of His right and dominion over the earth to His people, that we too would have power over the devil.

We inflate the devil's power through our ignorance. We give him power where he did not possess it. Do not think for a minute that he will not take advantage of you when you give him this power. Remember that He is defeated and he cannot harm you.

Do you want to express the brilliance of God's glory? Open those protective areas in your life to God's Holy Spirit. Understand the power of God's inheritance. Understand the power of God's life in you. Understand the enemy is defeated and quit giving him power where he does not possess power. To whom ever I make myself a slave, I am a slave.

God never intended His people to be a whiny sniffling nosed bunch of defeated people. Look at the lives of the apostles. They were triumphant unto death. Do you think that we might be living in a time where being a Christian can kill you? We are. So what? God made us MORE than conquerors through His Son.

Stand up and start fighting! Take your sword, take you shield, put on the armor of God and get into the fight! Take what was the devil's and deliver it to Christ as part of His kingdom. Do the work that God called you to do. Do not despair, do not whine, do not murmur, be brave, be of good courage and fear not. God is on your right and on your left, He is your rear guard, He gave you power to destroy the works of the devil. He made you a light that would draw others unto Him. Become more brilliant—give God more of yourself.

Walking in the Light

> *I John 1:5 This is the message we have heard from him and proclaim to you, that God is light and in him is no darkness at all.*

God is light and He has called us all to walk in that light. What I want to discuss with you is what it means to walk in the light, how to get there and how to stay there. We will look at some of the benefits of walking in the light.

> *I John 1:7 but if we walk in the light, as he is in the light, we have fellowship with one another, and the blood of Jesus his Son cleanses us from all sin.*

The Physical

First, it is important to understand that we are in a physical existence. Our senses are earthy and our actions take physical movement. That is to say, most everything in our everyday experience is four-dimensional life (height, width, depth, and time). This has the tendency to force our thinking into a four-dimensional thinking.

What I mean by this is if we are going to be late for an appointment, we look for ways to get there on time, but never do we think of slowing down time to allow us the time to be there on time. Another example would be, we see a child pull in front of a car on his bicycle and we seek ways to save the child. We either yell and warn the child or try to warn the car to stop or try to get the child out of harm's way. Never do we consider grabbing hold of the car and bringing it to a stop. The car is much bigger then we are and we know that we cannot stop it.

The laws of our physical universe condition our minds to operate within the confines of these physical laws. This creates a physical minded mentality. However, in reality we are not confined to the physical laws as Christians. We have been delivered from physical minded mentality and the walls that separated our minds from dreaming the impossible have been destroyed.

The Spiritual

We are so used to our physical universe that we forget that we are spiritual beings with houses of flesh. Our flesh represents our physical universe and all the limitations that its laws place upon us. Our spirit man, however, is not of this physical world; it is in the likeness of its Father, who is God. Your mother and father can only be the mother and father of your body, but God fashioned a spirit to inhabit that body. We see our flesh so much that we forget that there is a spirit man at the controls of it. When you look into the mirror, you cannot see your spirit, but you do see your flesh and that is what you are comfortable with because that is what is familiar to you.

To illustrate our spiritual nature I usually ask people where their memory is located. Most respond that it is located in our brains. Let us think this out. If it were located in our brains, then when our brain died so would our memory. We would be standing before God with no identity or know what our life was like or what we did. We would not know where we had come from nor would we know any of our relatives that had gone before us. We would just be a blank slate of being with no knowledge of anything. We know from Scripture that this is not so.

Look at the account of the rich man and Lazarus. After they had both died, the rich man called to Abraham to have Lazarus, whom he knew while alive, to dip his finger in water to soothe his torment. We have to conclude then that our memory is not actually in our physical being but in our spiritual being.

Since our memory is spiritual, we have to access it through our brain to bring it from the spiritual realm into the physical realm, and it is the limitations of our brain that affect what we can bring consciously to remembrance. I would argue that each of us will have perfect recall when we shed the limitations of our physical being. Therefore, when we stand before the Creator, we will know all things regarding our lives.

What happened when you became a Christian? Your spirit was reconciled back into fellowship with God. You now have communion with God and He with you. God wanted us to understand the fullness of what this means so He gave us an example—Jesus.

Jesus showed that He was not subject to the physical laws in the many miracles that He performed. He healed the sick, raised the dead, walked on water, was transfigured, knew the hearts of others, made wine from water, and fed 5,000 people with a boy's lunch. Jesus said something interesting, He said, *"the works that I do, you shall do too, and greater works then these shall you do."* Whoa! You mean He was talking about doing miracles?

Yes, He was talking about miracles. If you study the gospels, you will find that Jesus called His miracles, *"works."* This is not an isolated incident of this teaching either. Jesus told us that if we have faith the size of a mustard seed, that when it is grown we could command a mountain to be uprooted and cast into the sea and it would obey. God has been trying to encourage us to think beyond the physical and enter into the kingdom of light where He dwells.

Fleshly Minded

We are all so used to thinking in limited terms that we apply these limitations to our lives. So many Christians are bound up in fleshly-minded mentality that emotional bonds of hurt and mistrust bind them. Most Christians that I have met have very deep hurts and issues stemming from the hurt perpetrated on them by loved ones.

One of the biggest scourges in the Body of Christ is poor self-esteem. Christians fight with this daily and fail because they are fleshly minded. Another scourge in the Body of Christ is pride. Now these two problems are at opposite ends of the scale. On the one end is a poor self-esteem and on the other is egotism.

In the 1980's we witnessed a big movement to address poor self-esteem in our children through programs initiated in our public schools; the goal was to increase a child's self-esteem. In the mid 1990's a report came out in USA Today that said these programs were indeed curing children of their poor self- esteem, but the problem was that they were now ego maniacs, full of themselves and selfish.

According to the psychologists, we should all be somewhere in the middle of that scale between poor self-esteem and high self-esteem. Well, that seems reasonable, but once we get in the middle of that scale, any deviation from the middle is a turn for the worse.

The man who is on the high end of the scale and is egotistical says, *"I do not need or want God."* The man who is on the low end of the scale and sees no worth in his self says, *"God does not need or want me."* Can you see the work of Satan in this? This should make you mad. Mad that you have been living a life hidden from the light because of the tricks of the enemy to get you to see yourself through other's eyes rather than God's eyes.

While walking in the light there is no fear or worry. There is no concern for the life of the flesh. This is so because you are accessing the super-natural realm of the Spirit where God dwells. Look at the examples that we have before us.

When Daniel was cast into the hungry lion's den, he was not showing fear, and he was protected. When the three Hebrew children were cast into the fiery furnace, they were not showing fear, and they were protected. When the apostles were cast into prison, there were not showing fear, and they were protected. They were walking in the light. It was not the lack of fear that protected them, but the presence of faith. They all were in the realization that their life was in the hands of God and there was no fear of death or even being hurt. Faith in God delivered them by way of their walk.

What Will Happen When You Walk in the Light?

> *Matthew 5:14-16* "*You are the light of the world. A city set on a hill cannot be hid. Nor do men light a lamp and put it under a bushel, but on a stand, and it gives light to all in the house. Let your light so shine before men, that they may see your good works and give glory to your Father who is in heaven.*

You are called by Jesus, "*the light of the world.*" Jesus fully expects us to walk in the light and become light. Why? So that others would see our good works and give glory unto God. Believing the Word of God causes you to walk in the light, and that changes your behavior.

> *Romans 13:12* *the night is far gone, the day is at hand. Let us then cast off the works of darkness and put on the armor of light;*

> *I John 2:9-11* *He who says he is in the light and hates his brother is in the darkness still. He who loves his brother abides in the light, and in it there is no cause for stumbling. But he who hates his brother is in the darkness and walks in the darkness, and does not know where he is going, because the darkness has blinded his eyes.*

When we walk in the light, we will not stumble. We do not stumble because we are walking according to what God has said.

When we walk according to what God has said, we align ourselves with reality and aligning ourselves with reality allows us to walk in truth, and walking in the truth is walking in the light.

Communicating With God

Prayer at its most simplistic definition is a communication directed toward God. However, it is not supposed to be a singly directed conversation. God indeed speaks to His own and in order to hear Him, we must tune ourselves to hear Him. The most rewarding times of prayer for me are when I would ask God a question and He would answer. It is much like a conversation between a child and a parent.

The man who prays ceases to be a fool, while the man who refuses to pray nourishes a blind life within his own brain and he will find no way out that road.
-- Chambers, O. (1996, c1931). Baffled to fight better: Talks on the Book of Job.

Prayer is often seen as a chore. How foolish! Prayer is a privilege to be cherished. How would you like a god to whom you could not cry out to, or a god to whom you could not express your deepest feelings of love, gratitude, hurts, disappointments, successes or triumphs? How would you like a god who refuses to listen to you, or a god who listens, but will not respond? That is not the God we serve! We Christians take the privilege of prayer too lightly. We need to understand prayer so that we will want to pray.

Prayer

As is often the case, the first thing necessary to understand a concept is first to understand the terms. It is for this reason that we must go to the original languages to get a picture for which we are in discussion so that understanding might take place. We have three major words used for prayer in the Old Testament.

Definition – *Prayer 1*

Hebrew - *palal /paw·**lal***

פָּלַל ...*in the derived nouns it has the meaning of judging, which is supposed to be derived from that of cutting, deciding, by comparison; to decide; but* فَلَّ *itself is i.q.* פָּרַר *to break.*

I prefer to regard the primary power of the root to be that of rolling, revolving, wallen, rollen (comp. פּוֹל, פָּלַל, פָּלַךְ, פָּלַשׁ, *Syr.* فَلَهَا *to roll in any thing, hence to tinge, to stain), hence to make even by rolling, to level with a roller (comp.* פָּלַס *to roll, walzen), whence to lay even (a cause), to arbitrate,*

***Piel.**—(1) to judge, 1 Sa. 2:25; also, to execute judgment in punishing, Ps. 106:30; compare Nu. 25:7 (LXX. and Vulg. however, to pacify; see under Kal). Followed by* לְ *to adjudge to any one, Eze. 16:52.*

Page | 161

(2) to think, to suppose, Gen. 48:11.

Hithpael.—*(1) to intercede for any one (prop. to interpose as mediator); followed by* בְּ *Deu. 9:20; 1 Sa. 7:5;* עַל *Job 42:8;* לְ *1 Sa. 2:25, id.; followed by* אֶל *of him to whom one intercedes and supplicates, Gen. 20:17; Nu. 11:2.*
(2) Generally to supplicate, to pray,
--Gesenius' Hebrew and Chaldee lexicon to the Old Testament Scriptures

The picture or sense behind this word is to make a decision between two positions and then entreat the judge on behalf of something or someone. *"To make even..."* has the idea of justice. Therefore, prayer from the Hebrew sense of this word is that heaven is the great courtroom where all justice is dispensed. To pray is to entreat the Judge to do justice or to show mercy.

For instance, when you pray for a fellow believer to be healed of a sickness, you are actually asking the Judge to show justice because the position of the Christian is that they are on the blessing side of the Law. Therefore, it is an act of justice to have that sickness removed since sickness is a curse of the Law.

On the other hand, if you were to pray for an unbeliever to be healed, you are asking the Judge of heaven to show mercy upon them because they are on the cursing side of the Law and their sickness is legal. Everything that you pray for is a judgment that asks either for mercy or for justice. With this in mind, consider the following:

> **Ezekiel 22:30-31** *"I searched for a man among them who would build up the wall and stand in the gap before Me for the land, so that I would not*

destroy it; but I found no one. ' Thus I have poured out My indignation on them; I have consumed them with the fire of My wrath; their way I have brought upon their heads,' declares the Lord God."

God was looking for someone to ask for His mercy. Because there was no one who would ask for mercy, He the Righteous Judge had to do justice to the land that resulted in the destruction of that nation.

> **Psalm 106:23** *Therefore He said that He would destroy them, Had not Moses His chosen one stood in the breach before Him, To turn away His wrath from destroying them.*

How many times have we underestimated our influence to bring mercy and to turn away the wrath of God from a person, a city, or a nation? When we look at the prayers of the saints in the Bible, we see this as a pattern. They literally saw God as Judge who would have to answer if they brought their case before Him. If we would again see God as Judge, would that not cause us to go before Him to plead our cause? Read II Chronicles 6:12-42. This is Solomon's prayer at the dedication of the new Temple. Look at how he entreats God. He speaks to God as the Judge.

Definition – *Prayer 2*

Hebrew - *athar /aw·thar*

I. עָתַר fut. יֶעְתַּר—(1) i.q. קָטַר to burn incense to a god, to smoke with perfume, incense; Arab. to breathe odours).

(2) to pray as a suppliant, to pray to a god (the prayers of the godly being compared to incense; -- Gesenius' Hebrew and Chaldee lexicon to the Old Testament Scriptures

This Hebrew word is mostly associated with repentance and the asking of forgiveness. The idea of incense is a picture of pleasant odors rising up to the Creator causing God to take notice and to show mercy. There is still another sense to this word though.

> **Revelation 8:3-5** *Another angel came and stood at the altar, holding a golden censer; and much **incense** was given to him, so that he might add it to the prayers of all the saints on the golden altar which was before the throne. And the smoke of the incense, with the prayers of the saints, went up before God out of the angel's hand. Then the angel took the censer and filled it with the fire of the altar, and threw it to the earth; and there followed peals of thunder and sounds and flashes of lightning and an earthquake.*

Intercession leaves you neither time nor inclination to pray for your own 'sad sweet self.' The thought of yourself is not kept out, because it is not there to keep out; you are completely and entirely identified with God's interests in other lives.
--- Chambers, O. (1993, c1935). My Utmost For His Highest

This picture in heaven tells us much about our prayers. Note first, that we cannot rely upon our individual prayers only to accomplish the will of God in the earth concerning certain things.

There must be corporate unity in prayer. Second, it was only when the incense of God, representing His judgment concerning those prayers, was added to them it resulted in the fire of God being poured out upon the earth. This was a depiction of God hearing the case and making a judgment.

Another interesting note is the Greek root word for incense. It is *"kill."* We must be willing to lay ourselves upon the altar of sacrifice that will release our prayers as incense before God.

The altar of incense in the tabernacle was to be located directly in front of the veil that was separating the Holy Place from the Most Holy Place. Therefore, that altar was directly in front of the throne or mercy seat of God. Remember that the veil has been removed through the body of Jesus. We can now enter boldly before the throne by our prayers to make our petitions known.

> **Hebrews 4:16** *Therefore let us draw near with confidence to the throne of grace, so that we may receive mercy and find grace to help in time of need.*

Another thing that needs to be noted is that only the priests were allowed to offer incense before the throne of God. Now we are all priests before our God. We are all commissioned to temple service since God dwells in you and you are the temple of the Holy Spirit.

Definition – *Prayer 3*

Hebrew – *tsâla' /tsel·aw*

צָלָה *to roast, 1 Sa. 2:15; Isa. 44:16. (Arab. id. The signification of roasting and praying (see Chaldee) are referred to the common notion of warmth by Schult. on Har. i. p. 25, to that of softening by Jo. Simonis, in Lex.) Hence* צָלִי. *--Gesenius' Hebrew and Chaldee lexicon to the Old Testament Scriptures*

This Hebrew word is only used twice. It has the sense of continual prayer. It is a prayer that is not quickly entered into nor quickly finished. It is prayer that is slowly roasted before God.

Prayer should never be used as an excuse not to witness. How many times have we said, *"Oh I will pray for that person."* Rather we should be praying **with them**. Praying with people brings the kingdom of God to the marketplace.

Jesus wants us to take His kingdom to the marketplace. We have been so conditioned by the secularists to be embarrassed to display our faith publicly that we have hidden ourselves away where no one can see us or hear us. God is calling us to awaken from our slumber and take God's kingdom to work with us. God will give us opportunities. The question is will we take them?

We need to see every opportunity as a span of time that has a beginning and an end. When the time is passed, we will never get it back. If we do not take advantage of that moment, it is lost forever. If that is not daunting enough, it is also possible that some of the people we refused to minister to could be lost as well. Will we be strong enough to minister in the marketplace? If we are ever to start praying with people, we need to understand how to do so effectively. That is why discipleship is so important.

> *When a man is at his wits' end it is not a cowardly thing to pray, it is the only way he can get into touch with Reality. Be yourself before God and present your problems, the things you know you have come to your wits' end over. As long as you are selfsufficient, you do not need to ask God for anything.*
> *-- Chambers, O. (1993, c1935). My utmost for his highest*

Prayer Dynamics

Prayer dynamics are those effects or conditions that are needed to produce prayer that produces effects. This is known as **effectual prayer**. By understanding what is needed when we pray we can expect to see results from prayer when we meet the conditions. I want to express a caution though.

We cannot formulize nor over spiritualize how to pray. Individual prayer needs to be fluid and dynamic. It needs to be spontaneous and fresh. It needs to be real and honest. Remember, you are unique before your God, so copying another's style of prayer because it worked for them is not going to work for you.

Conditions For Effective Prayer

There are certain conditions that need to exist for us to pray effectively. It is dutiful for us then to understand these conditions and seek to meet them in order to be effectual in prayer.

The first condition for effective prayer is faith.

> **Hebrews 11:6** *And without faith it is impossible to please Him, for he who comes to God must believe that He is and that He is a rewarder of those who seek Him.*

It is obvious that it is necessary to believe in God before we come to Him in prayer. We must also believe that He will hear us and answer our prayers. Why else would we pray unless we were just doing an experiment? Some people just try prayer to see if it will work. That is not a prayer of faith. Even in this, God has sometimes answered to give that person a chance to believe. Yet, if they will not enter into belief, they will not have what they ask for from God.

> **James 5:14-15** *Is anyone among you sick? Then he must call for the elders of the church and they are to pray over him, anointing him with oil in the name of the Lord; and the **prayer offered in faith** will restore the one who is sick, and the Lord will raise him up, and if he has committed sins, they will be forgiven him.*

If we do not believe that we will receive from the Lord, we are deluding ourselves in prayer. We start hoping that God will hear us, and then we start hoping that He will answer us. In the end, we do not receive because we did not believe.

> **James 1:5-7** *But if any of you lacks wisdom, let him ask of God, who gives to all generously and without reproach, and it will be given to him. **But he must***

ask in faith without any doubting, for the one who doubts is like the surf of the sea, driven and tossed by the wind. For that man ought not to expect that he will receive anything from the Lord,

Your Father wants you to **expect** to receive. In fact, He wants you to believe that He is so faithful with your prayer that you actually believe that you have received it at the moment you ask. Therefore, it is your doubt that is the thief of manifestation. God knows our hearts. We are unable to escape the eyes of the Lord. We deceive ourselves if we think we are fooling God.

Determination

Luke 18:1-8 Now He was telling them a parable **to show that at all times they ought to pray and not to lose heart,** *saying, "In a certain city there was a judge who did not fear God and did not respect man. "There was a widow in that city, and she kept coming to him, saying, 'Give me legal protection from my opponent.' "For a while he was unwilling; but afterward he said to himself, 'Even though I do not fear God nor respect man, yet because this widow bothers me, I will give her legal protection, otherwise by continually coming she will wear me out.' " And the Lord said, "Hear what the unrighteous judge said; now, will not God bring about justice for His elect who cry to Him day and night, and will He delay long over them? "I tell you that He will bring about justice for them quickly. However, when the Son of Man comes, will He find faith on the earth?"*

The idea of this parable is **not** that you are bothering God when you pray. It is about a contrast. The contrast is that of an evil judge and the Righteous Judge. If an evil judge will do what is right because of many petitions from the same person, what will the Righteous Judge from heaven do on your behalf?

The question in verse eight *(When the Son of Man comes, will He find faith in the earth?)* needs to be addressed. What is meant by this question? Is it that man will be so exacerbated by the time their needs are addressed that they will lose faith? That does not seem to be the case since just before that He declares that God will bring about justice quickly.

This is what I think Jesus is trying to convey. If we really believe that God is the Righteous Judge that will hear our case and speedily reply, we have faith. Nevertheless, if we are wishy-washy in our belief about God's faithfulness to hear and act, we lack faith which causes us not to act. If we really believe that God is a Righteous Judge, then we will be determined in our petition until we receive the answer. If we do not believe that, we will not petition often.

> *Luke 11:5-9 Then He said to them, "Suppose one of you has a friend, and goes to him at midnight and says to him, 'Friend, lend me three loaves; for a friend of mine has come to me from a journey, and I have nothing to set before him'; and from inside he answers and says, 'Do not bother me; the door has already been shut and my children and I are in bed; I cannot get up and give you anything.' "I tell you, even though he will not get up and give him anything because he is his friend, yet because of his persistence he will get up and give him as much as he needs. "So I say to you, ask, and it will be given*

to you; seek, and you will find; knock, and it will be opened to you.

Again, the idea of being determined to pray into that which you need, is what is being presented. It is not the repetition that is moving God; it is a persistence in faith. Faith demands action. Therefore, if you have faith, you will not faint in praying for that which you are having faith. It will move you to continue to make declarations in accordance to the promise upon which you are standing.

A Clean Heart

> *I Timothy 2:8 Therefore I want the men in every place to pray, lifting up holy hands, without wrath and dissension.*

Many a Christian thinks that they can hold anger, unforgiveness, and dissension and still think that God will hear them. God wants you to approach Him with your heart clean.

> *Mark 11:25 "Whenever you stand praying, forgive, if you have anything against anyone, so that your Father who is in heaven will also forgive you your transgressions.*

Alertness

> *Luke 21:36 "But keep on the alert at all times, praying that you may have strength to escape all these things that are about to take place, and to stand before the Son of Man."*

The Greek word for *"alert"* means to watch. We need to have the attitude of watching and being ready to do what our King asks of us to do. Notice that being alert means that you are praying. Praying is a sign of being watchful.

Attitude Of Dialogue

> *I Thessalonians 5:17 pray without ceasing;*

Remember that prayer is communication between God and man. To pray without ceasing is always to be of the mind that God can interrupt you at any time. There must be open dialogue with God at all times. This means that you take God with you everywhere you go.

Prayer Instructions

We need to take heed of some instructions concerning prayer. There must be purpose in praying for certain things based upon the instruction of the Word. Let us look at prayer instructions.

Pray While the Lord is Near

> *Psalm 32:6 Therefore, let everyone who is godly pray to You in a time when You may be found; Surely in a flood of great waters they will not reach him.*

The idea here is to pray at a time of rest and safety and to be repentant now. If we do not, then calamity will come and it is too late to pray. Not that it is too late to pray for repentance, but that calamity came because I did not pray for repentance.

Pray For the Peace of Jerusalem

Psalm 122:6 *Pray for the peace of Jerusalem: "May they prosper who love you.*

Pray For Those Who Persecute You

Matthew 5:44 *"But I say to you, love your enemies and pray for those who persecute you,*

Do Not Pray to be Heard or Seen

Matthew 6:5-6 *"When you pray, you are not to be like the hypocrites; for they love to stand and pray in the synagogues and on the street corners so that they may be seen by men. Truly I say to you, they have their reward in full. "But you, when you pray, go into your inner room, close your door and pray to your Father who is in secret, and your Father who sees what is done in secret will reward you.*

Do Not Use Repetition When Praying

Matthew 6:7 *"And when you are praying, do not use meaningless repetition as the Gentiles do, for they suppose that they will be heard for their many words.*

Pray to Not Enter Into Temptation

Matthew 26:41 *"Keep watching and praying that you may not enter into temptation; the spirit is willing, but the flesh is weak."*

Do Not Be Results Oriented

When you are results oriented, you are showing your lack of faith and you are waiting for the manifestation before you believe. Faith says it is done before you see it.

> *If we only look for results in the earthlies when we pray, we are ill-taught. A praying saint performs far more havoc amongst the unseen forces of darkness than we have the slightest notion of.*
> *-- Chambers, O. (1996). Biblical psychology : A treasure Chest for Christian Counselors.*

Mark 11:24 *"Therefore I say to you, all things for which you pray and ask, believe that you have received them, and they will be granted you.*

II Corinthians 1:20 *For as many as are the promises of God, in Him they are yes; therefore also through Him is our Amen to the glory of God through us.*

This means that God has already performed His promises. Therefore, if I ask Him something that He has promised, He has already said yes to me. I do not have to wonder if He will perform it. I know He will perform it. This is why it also says that through Him is our Amen. Amen is a Hebrew word *("aman")* that means faithful. He is faithful and His faithfulness allows us to believe that He has already said "yes" to us regarding His promises.

Prayer Environments

There are different environments under which we pray. There are the external environments of private, public, single and corporate prayer. Then there are the internal environments of intercession, prayer burdens, thanksgiving, and supplications.

External – Private

> **Matthew 6:6** "*But you, when you pray, go into your inner room, close your door and pray to your Father who is in secret, and your Father who sees what is done in secret will reward you.*

We are to set aside times to get alone with the Lord to pray. This is where you can pour out your inner most secrets unto God. Note that there is also an open reward for this type of prayer. When you go into secret to pray, you are not praying in order to be heard or seen. It is just out of a desire to be with your Heavenly Father. Your Father will answer and reward you.

External – Public

When praying in public we have already seen the instruction that we are not pray in order to be seen or heard of men. There are times we have to pray in public, but it should be to the glory of God not to the glory of yourself.

There must be mention also of the benefit of corporate prayer. When we come together to pray in one accord, we are able to super charge the results. The allusion to this is found in the Scriptures.

> ***Leviticus 26:7-9*** *'But you will chase your enemies and they will fall before you by the sword; five of you will chase a hundred, and a hundred of you will chase ten thousand, and your enemies will fall before you by the sword. 'So I will turn toward you and make you fruitful and multiply you, and I will confirm My covenant with you.*

There is also the Scripture that, *"one shall put a hundred to flight and two a thousand."* In both cases, the increase is five fold. So at the very least we have a five fold increase in ability and power when we pray corporately in unity.

Internal – Intercession

Intercession is when you are standing in the gap between God and a person or people. This important type of prayer should not be confused with some of the ideas of spiritual warfare. You are not between demons and the person, but between God and the person.

> *Worship and intercession must go together, the one is impossible without the other. Intercession means that we rouse ourselves up to get the mind of Christ about the one for whom we pray.*
> *-- Chambers, O. (1993, c1935). My utmost for his highest*

> ***II Chronicles 7:14*** *and My people who are called by My name humble themselves and pray and seek*

My face and turn from their wicked ways, then I will
hear from heaven, will forgive their sin and will
heal their land.

The nations of this world are riding upon the blessings of God upon His people, the Christians. As we humble ourselves and pray, God will heal our land because we are interceding for it. Intercession is not fighting the devil in spiritual warfare; it is beseeching the Lord for His mercy upon another.

__Hebrews 7:25__ Therefore He is able also to save
forever those who draw near to God through Him,
since He always lives to make intercession for them.

Jesus is interceding for us. He stands between the throne of God and you. As you draw near to Him, He is able to intercede for you.

Internal – Supplication

Supplication is actually a cry for favor from God. It is a prayer that is asking God to do something on our behalf or on behalf of another that is not deserved.

__Zechariah 12:10__ "I will pour out on the house of
David and on the inhabitants of Jerusalem, the
Spirit of grace and of supplication, so that they will
look on Me whom they have pierced; and they will
mourn for Him, as one mourns for an only son, and
they will weep bitterly over Him like the bitter
weeping over a firstborn.

Prayer burdens many times are not understood and therefore not acted upon. It often starts with just a feeling that something is not right. We need to be sensitive to them because we are able to change the course of events in the lives of people or even nations. God knows all things. Nevertheless, He chooses to do His will through us, His people. When God wants to do something, He will give His servants a prayer burden so that they will begin to pray. As they pray, their faith releases God to act upon the burden that He gave them.

A good example of this is the following account. Kathryn, my wife, suddenly got a burden to pray. As she began to pray, she saw the state of Florida and a cloud like a sock was being pulled over the whole state as well as some of the states just north of it. We had no idea what the implication was, but we prayed until we felt the burden lift. The next day we were watching the news and a terrorist cell had been caught in Florida. They had blueprints of a nuclear power plant with access to that plant. They had planned to create a meltdown that could have affected the whole area.

So be listening for God to give you a prayer burden and make sure you pray until you feel the burden lift. Know that God is putting that same burden on other saints as well. As the combination of your prayers reach heaven, God is able to act on behalf of your prayers.

Internal – Thanksgiving

> **Philippians 4:6** *Be anxious for nothing, but in everything by prayer and supplication with*

thanksgiving let your requests be made known to God.

We are to be thankful at all times when we approach God on His throne. A heart of thankfulness is also a heart of faith. It is thankful for it knows that it has what is asked for because God is faithful.

> **Colossians 4:2** *Devote yourselves to prayer, keeping alert in it with an attitude of thanksgiving;*

> **I Timothy 2:1-3** *First of all, then, I urge that entreaties and prayers, petitions and thanksgivings, be made on behalf of all men, for kings and all who are in authority, so that we may lead a tranquil and quiet life in all godliness and dignity. This is good and acceptable in the sight of God our Savior,*

Pray For Divine Intervention

Many times the Spirit of God will give us instructions. Sometimes these instructions seem impossible to us. It is at this point that we should pray and ask God to open a door so that we are able to fulfill His instructions.

Praying in the Spirit

We could not conclude our chapter on prayer without mentioning praying in the spirit. I want to thank Prophet John Kolb of *Clarion Call Ministries* in Post Falls, Idaho for helping me solidify the doctrines concerning this issue. First, we need to define what is praying in the Spirit.

I Corinthians 14:14-15 For if I pray in a tongue, my spirit prays, but my mind is unfruitful. What is the outcome then? I will pray with the spirit and I will pray with the mind also; I will sing with the spirit and I will sing with the mind also.

Paul describes two types of prayer. Praying with my mind and praying with my spirit. The only way I can pray with my spirit is to pray in tongues. In this way my mind is unfruitful. In other words, my mind has no idea what is being prayed. However, we do have some indication what is being prayed.

I Corinthians 14:2 For one who speaks in a tongue does not speak to men but to God; for no one understands, but in his spirit he speaks mysteries.

You are speaking mysteries unto God. Mysteries are simply things that are hidden.

I Corinthians 14:16-17 Otherwise if you bless in the spirit only, how will the one who fills the place of the ungifted say the "Amen" at your giving of thanks, since he does not know what you are saying? For you are giving thanks well enough, but the other person is not edified.

You are giving thanks unto God.

Acts 2:11 Cretans and Arabs—we hear them in our own tongues speaking of the mighty deeds of God."

You are speaking of the mighty deeds of God.

Acts 10:46 For they were hearing them speaking with tongues and exalting God. Then Peter answered,

You are speaking exultations unto God.

Romans 8:26-27 In the same way the Spirit also helps our weakness; for we do not know how to pray as we should, but the Spirit Himself intercedes for us with groanings too deep for words; and He who searches the hearts knows what the mind of the Spirit is, because He intercedes for the saints according to the will of God.

You are allowing the Spirit of God to use your spirit to intercede for the saints.

Jude 20 But you, beloved, building yourselves up on your most holy faith, praying in the Holy Spirit,

Here the importance of praying in the Spirit is likened to the importance of building up your faith. I believe that we could also make an inference here to the idea that faith is built up by praying in the Spirit. Not that it is sustained, for that can only take place through the Word of God. Rather that it is a temporary infusion of faith as I pray in the Spirit. The next time you find yourself in a difficult position, pray in the Spirit and watch your faith grow.

The next thing I want to address is the question, *"Is the gift of tongues for every believer?"* I believe it is. Let me preface this, however, with the statement that if someone does not speak in tongues it does not mean that they are less spiritual or that they lack the baptism of the Spirit. Spirituality is revealed through the fruits of the Spirit, not the gifts. Much of the damage that has been done to the reputation of the Pentecostal church has been over these very issues.

Let us explore this a moment. If the gifts of the Spirit are a result of being baptized in the Spirit, then any of the spiritual gifts are evidence of that baptism. For instance, if a person who does not speak in tongues prophecies, they are demonstrating evidence that they are baptized in the Spirit. The gift of tongues is not THE evidence but AN evidence of baptism.

The other thing that leads me to believe that this is a gift for all believers is that this is the only gift that edifies the individual speaking it. Another person speaking in tongues does not edify me, it edifies only them. Prophecy edifies the Church so anyone who prophecies can edify the Church. The gift of tongues is also called praying in the Spirit. Again, it makes sense that all would be able to pray in the Spirit.

I also want to clear up the Scripture where Paul states the rhetorical question, *"Do all speak in tongues?"* If the context of that question could be shown to be the local meeting then it is speaking about giving a message in tongues that is to be interpreted. Thus, here it does not refer to praying in the Spirit. If the context is outside the meeting, then it could be rendered a different way.

Everyone will have to study this and be convinced in his or her own hearts as to the context. If you look at the context of the last few verses of First Corinthians twelve, you will see that the context is the Body of Christ. We know that the Body of Christ can be spoken of as local or global. Therefore, whether it is global or local can change the meaning of Paul's rhetorical question. I think it does point to the local body.

What really needs to be addressed is that we should not let this issue divide us in any way. We should not use our position to demean or batter a person. Rather just make a convincing argument for your case. We should not look upon a person as less spiritual if they do not speak in tongues or more spiritual if they do; just as we should not think of someone more spiritual if they prophecy or less spiritual if they do not. Remember, God will not force something on someone and neither should we. We should exhort and encourage them to receive all that God has for them with gentleness and grace.

Conclusion

As you can see, prayer is very important, although we have treated it with a flippancy that is an embarrassment to us all. We really do not take some of the things of God with seriousness. We do not see the same importance being placed upon prayer and Bible reading that we used to see. We have been bantered into the belief that our faith is to remain private. When we see how so many human beings have been willing to give their lives for the cause of Christianity, we stand ashamed that we were unwilling to minister in the marketplace because it is unpopular or embarrassing.

Infuse yourselves again with the resolve that you will allow God to use you in the marketplace. I would hope that after reading and hearing this course, you are renewed again to the importance of prayer. Then having been renewed to it, you will engage in prayer again. After all, you are in communication with the Creator of the universe!

You might be thinking that this seems like an odd chapter to be placed in this book. After all, this book is about indentifying an answer to its title, *"Is God Calling You To Ministry?"* The purpose of this chapter is revealed in the following Scripture.

> **John 14:14** *"If you ask Me anything in My name, I will do it.*

You see, this promise was only spoken to one group of people. Read the context of chapters 13, 14, 15, and 16. It is instructions to His disciples. Therefore, this promise is not for just anyone. It is for those who have surrendered their lives to the call of God.

The answer to the question, *"Is God calling you to ministry?"* is a resounding, YES! If you would now take the next step by surrendering to that call and enter into discipleship to be equipped for it, you will be anointed and empowered to do the works of God. You will be able to ask Jesus anything in His name and He will do it!

About the Author

Bishop Mark Shaw and his wife Kathryn, are co-founders and directors of *Five Fold Ministries Training Academy (FFMTA)* and *Collegium Bible Institute* where the next generation of ministers is being equipped for God's service around the world. Bishop Shaw is the author of *"The Glory of Kings"* and *"The Government of God."* Shaw is the senior editor of *A Voice in the Wilderness* newsletter, which is published quarterly. He is also founder of Collegium Books, which is a publishing and distribution firm that seeks to offer educational materials for the equipping of the saints for the work of God. Shaw has been in ministry for thirty-two years. He was vice-director of Five Fold Ministries for twelve years and has been director for the last nine years. He also presides as pastor over *Adonai Worship Center* in Cannon Falls, Minnesota.

Shaw teaches on the structure and government of the Church with emphasis on divine order. He brings clarity to the Scripture by revealing a Hebraic understanding and emphasizes the causes and conditions upon which we develop our faith. His desire is to return true discipleship back to the Church so that true leaders are being forged with truth and integrity. He has a vision for the Church that is cutting edge and Spirit mandated.

In 2008 Shaw founded the Five Fold Ministries on-line E-learning center. The E-learning center is designed to distribute world class learning to students through internet technology that brings the school into the living room. The purpose is to develop leaders nationally and internationally that are willing to arrange the Church and its leaders in such a way that validates the Church as a voice in a secular society.

Called to the office of ministry, Kathryn Colton Shaw has a heart and a voice to teach those that are hungry to walk in the ways of the Lord, and awaken them to do what God has called them to do. It is Kathryn's desire to bring healing to the whole person in order that they may be released to accomplish the destiny for which they were created. Kathryn has a gift for networking and hosting seminars and educational programs. She is also gifted in administration and is a valuable asset in giving direction to the Church. Pastor Kathryn is the co-founder of *FFMTA* and *Collegium Bible Institute* where she serves as Academic Dean/Counselor and continues to develop curriculum to impact the next generation for Christ. The Shaws reside in Minnesota and they have six children and ten grandchildren that live in California and North Carolina.

Collegium Bible Institute
*The International Equipping School of the
Five Fold Ministry*

Collegium Bible Institute registers new students for the local campus every March. For more information on the ordination program at the local campus, write us at 410 Dakota Street W Cannon Falls, MN 55009 or call us at 888-808-5455. The website for the local campus is: www.collegiumbibleinstitute.com

If you are interested in the Online E-Learning Center visit us at: www.5fold.org

The Lord commanded His disciples to go into all the world and make disciples of all nations, teaching them to observe all that He said. The question then is, *"Have you been discipled yet?"*

Coming Soon April 2009

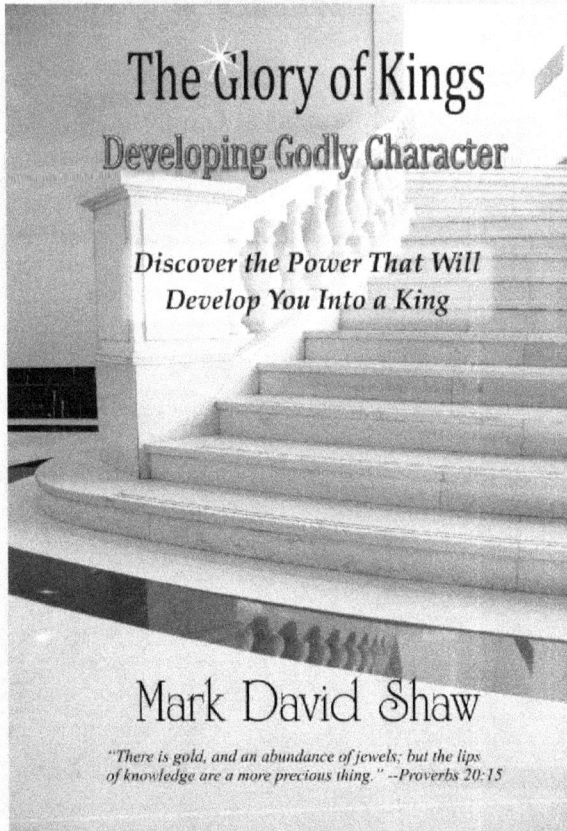

"It is the Glory of God to hide a thing and the Glory of Kings to search it out." – Proverbs 25:2

In developing godly character there is not the enforcement of the power of the will but a search for the Creator. We are brought to godly living through the exercise of our faith. God has planted His Word and we must nourish and grow it in our lives. Doing this has the wonderful effect of developing your character and it has the power of transforming you into the image of His Son.